anima

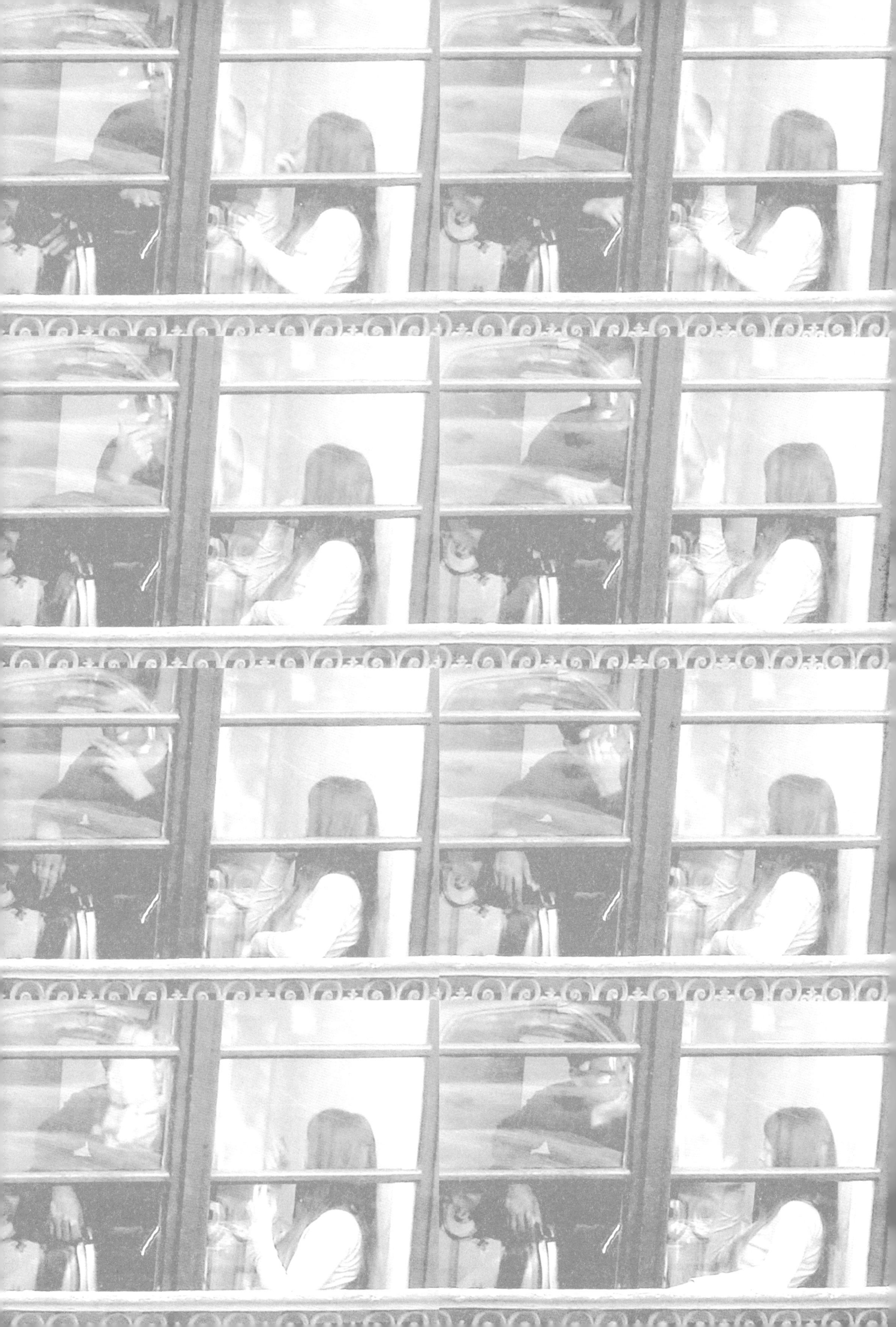

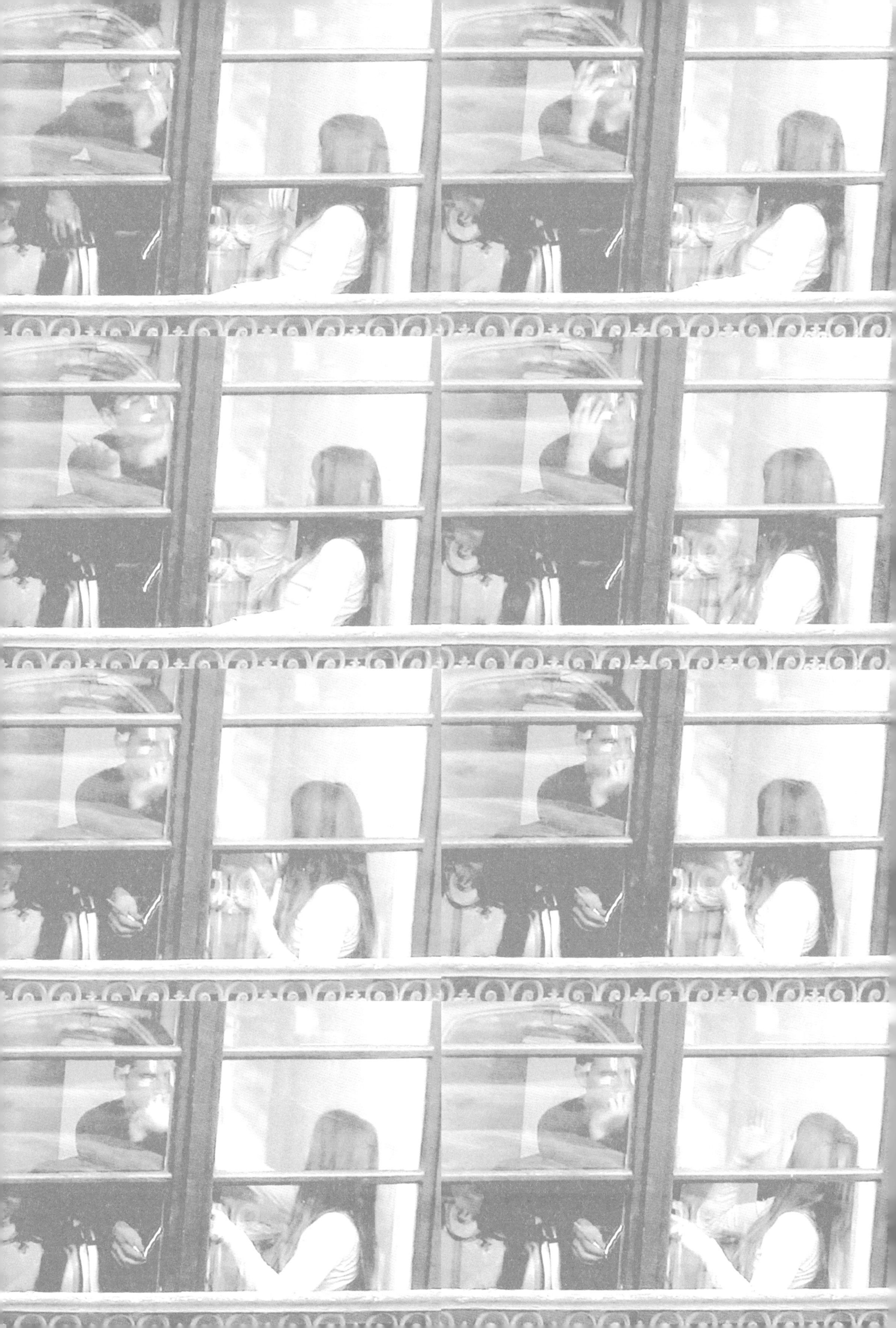

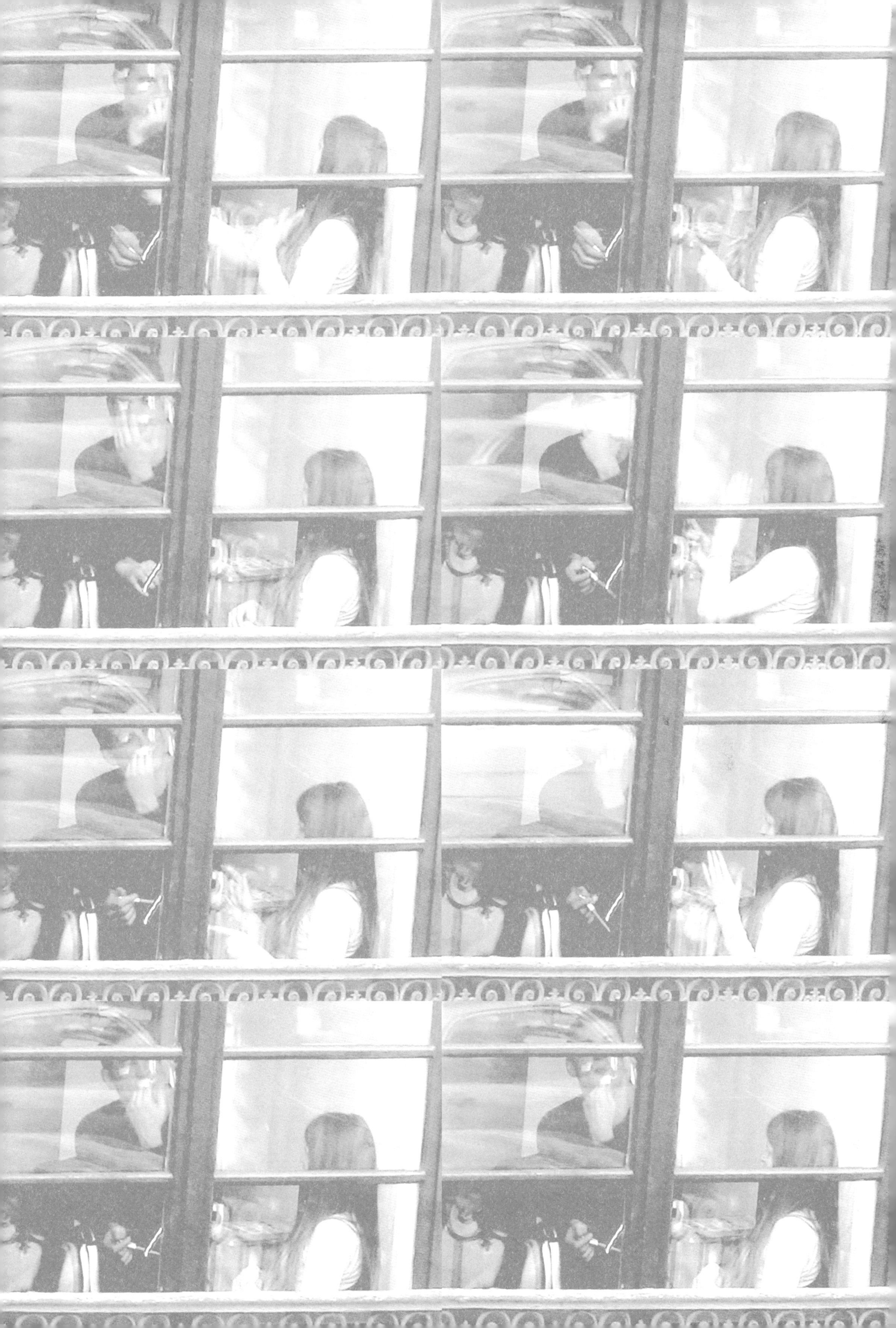

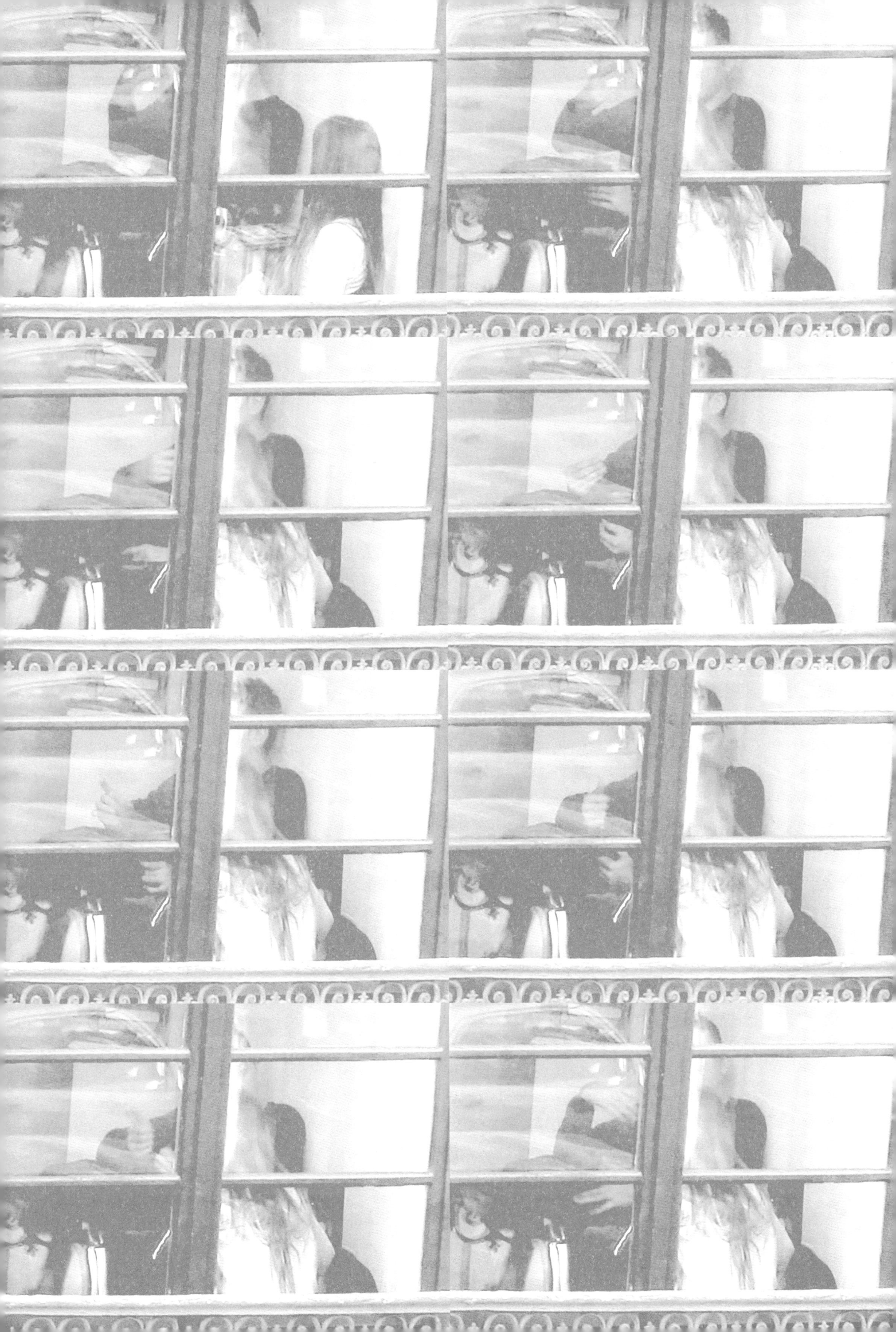

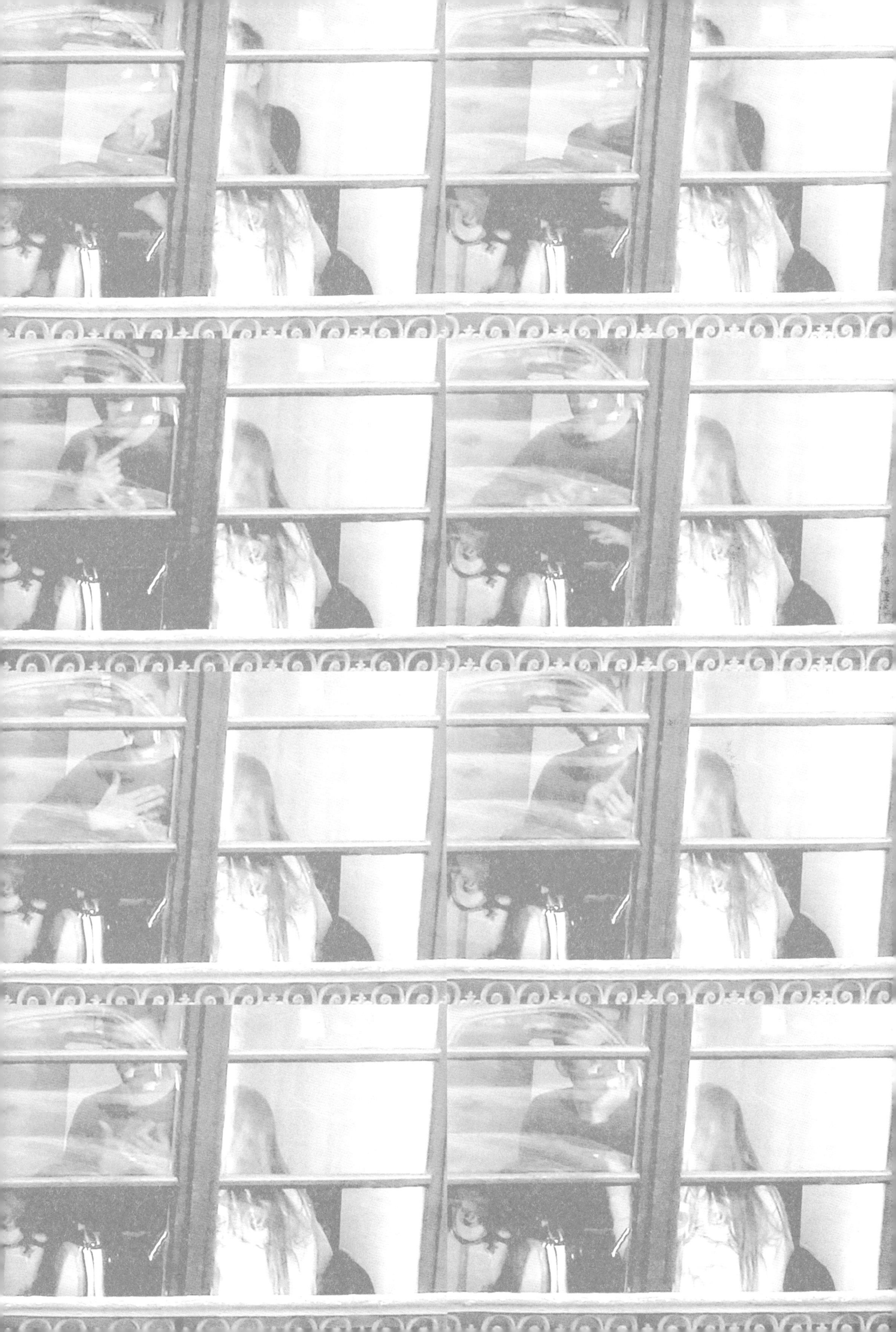

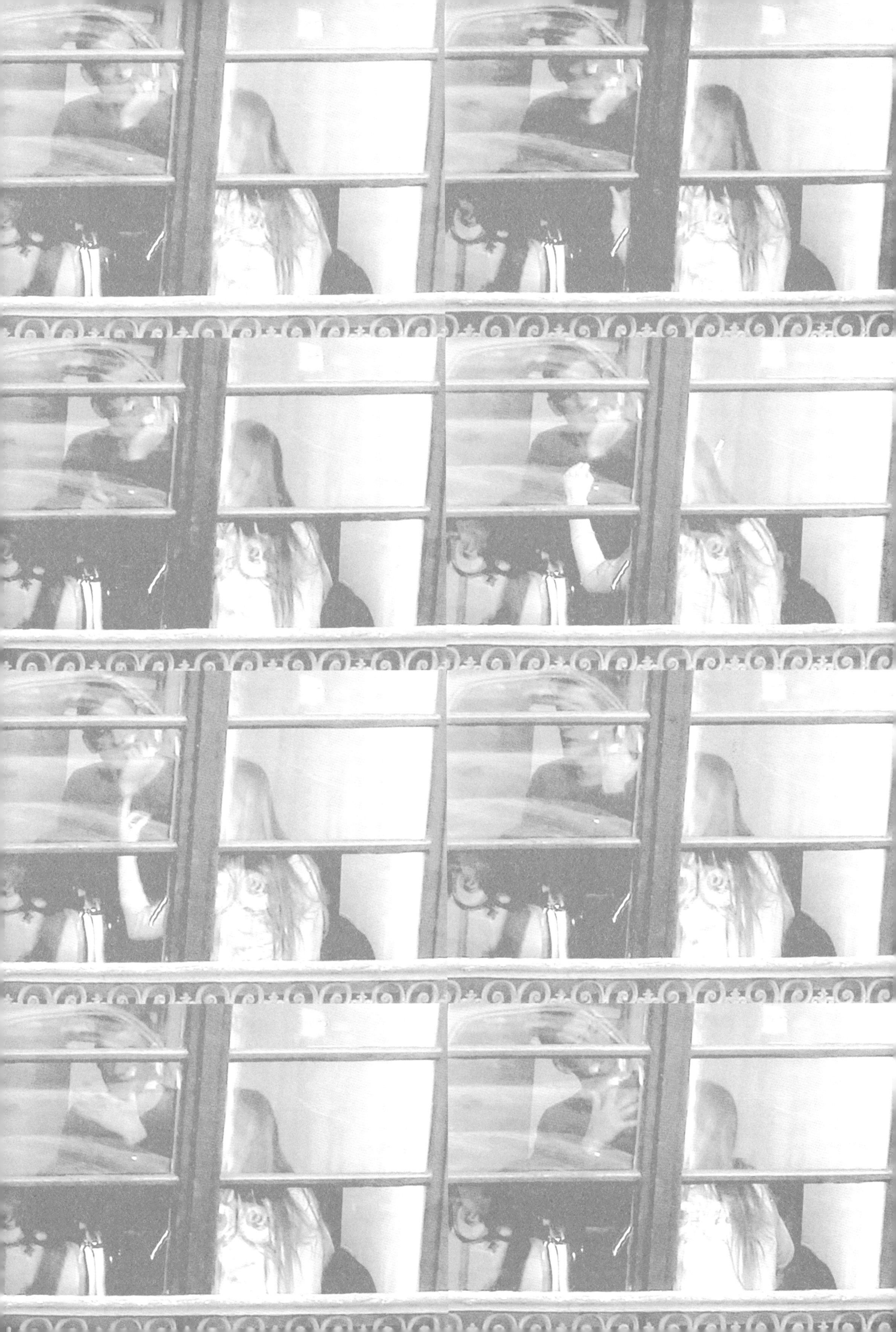

sometimes I dream that I'm an artist
            curators and admirers point and motion
                elaborately at my work
                    and in the same dream
                                        I get the appreciation I've always wanted to receive
                        in my dream I'm not just an artist
                    no, I'm a painter
                        but I'm an artist, not a painter
                            not even a sculptor, not even this

            why am I so frustrated
and why does it gnaw at my soul?
            why should the artist be a painter?
            am I the 'other' artist, are they inferior?
            do you know what fascinates me?

                                sometimes I want to stand so close to a painting
                that I might leave the condensation of my breath on the canvas
        not because I want to see or smell the paint
        I want to see what's not there anymore

but what once was, always has been
                    I want to see the hand
                        the hand that paints the gesture

                                        the hand in which you recognize the artist
                            the true artist
                the orator or the passionate artist

what am I? where is my hand?
                where do you recognize me in my work?

                        am I invisible?
                            where am I in my work?
                                where is my handprint?

no paint, no pressure on the brush, no gesture
                do you hear my story?
            can someone see what I want to say?
                        see me moving in space, in the studio
                            without clear direction
                                yet, with brush in hand

see me painting
        can you see me painting?
                a surface in the middle of the space
                        upright, well supported and stable
                                in blue, the blue of the sky

        or, at least the blue that I think the blue of the sky could be
        as if I'm painting air
in thin air

        I fear the gesture, or am I afraid to make a gesture?
                my hand moves from left to right and back again
                        confident, more confident than my movements before

                now close, eye, hand, surface
                absorbed and close
        the brush stops abruptly
        and falters, to turn back again
                lower, but still overlapping
                down, to the edge
                        do you see my gesture in that hesitation?

                                        in turning the hand
                                never the same, always different
                                the painting is there

but at the same time not
                see those brush strokes dissolve into the blue plane as it dries
                even the colour disappears
                the paint is dry

                                I take a step backwards
                I can't do more, that's all I can do
        subtly, only the edge distinguishes itself from the air
        the painting is gone, and at the same time the gesture?
am I not a painter after all?
my hand doesn't want to follow
                my hand falters

                                        doubts
                                        I would love to be a painter

fortissimo

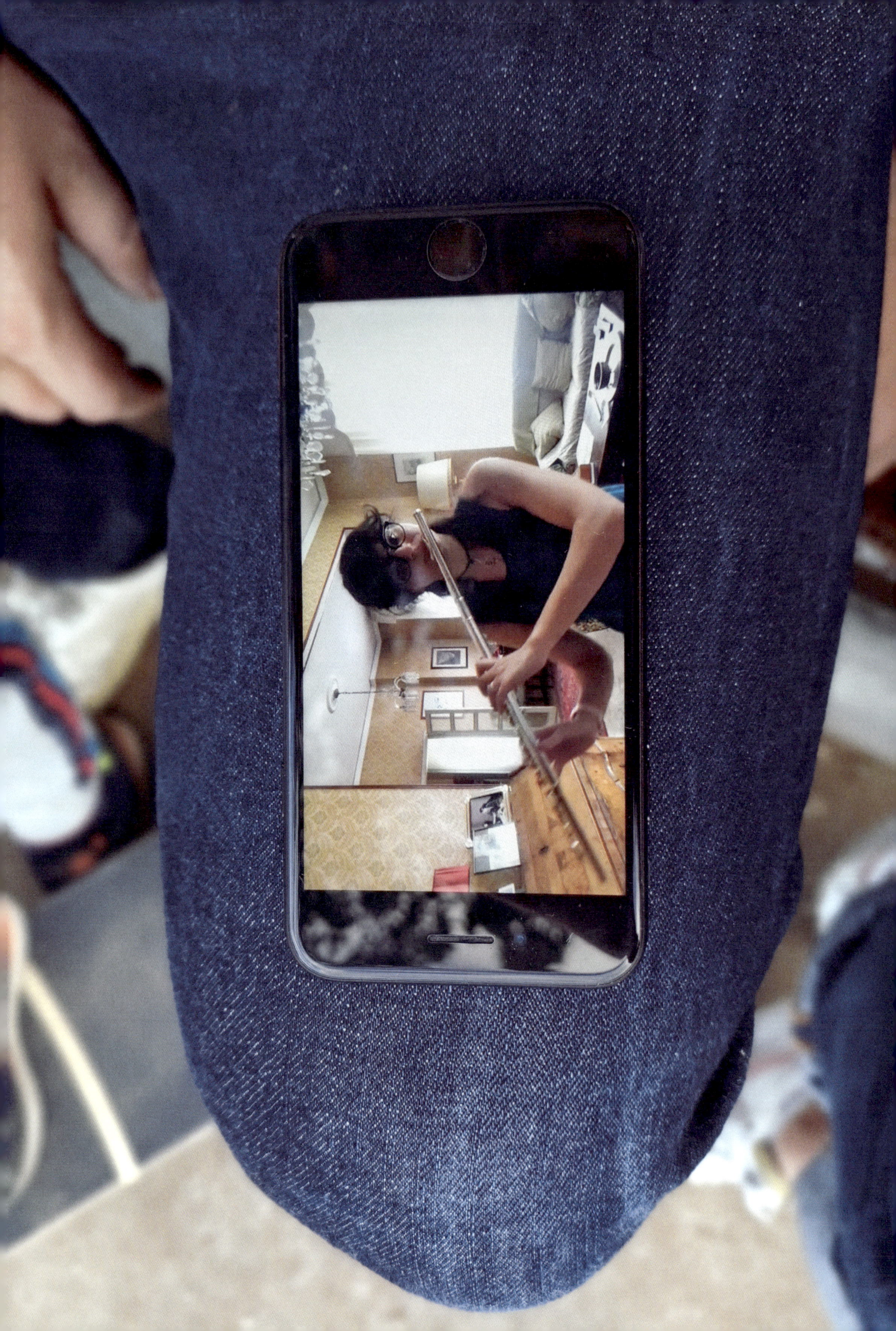

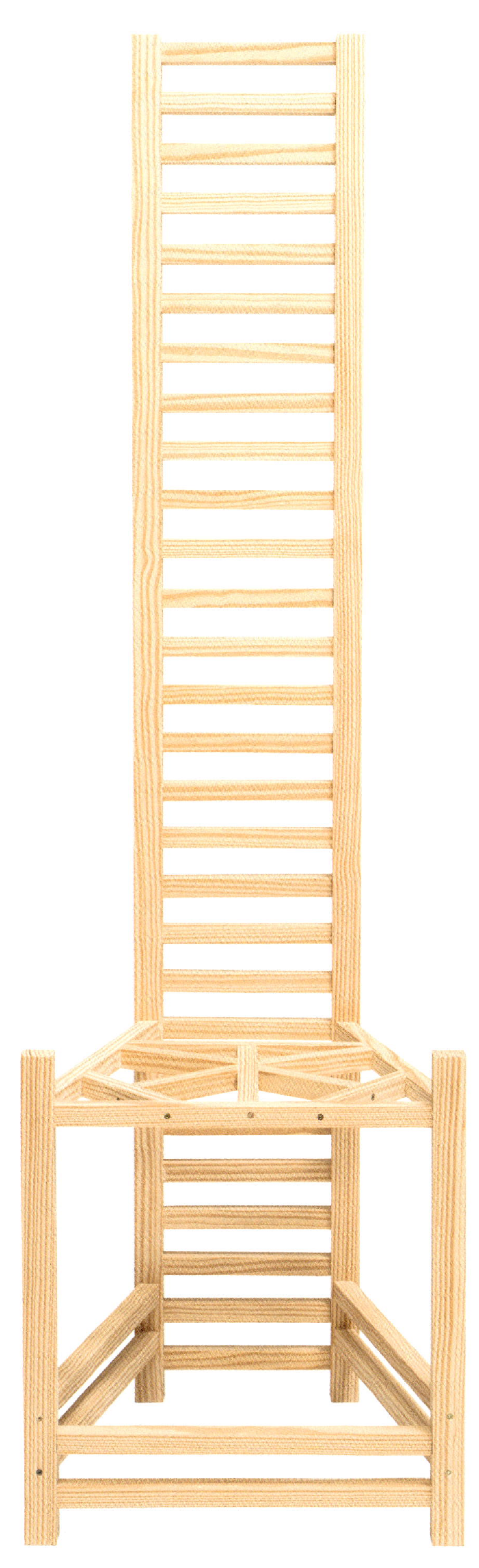

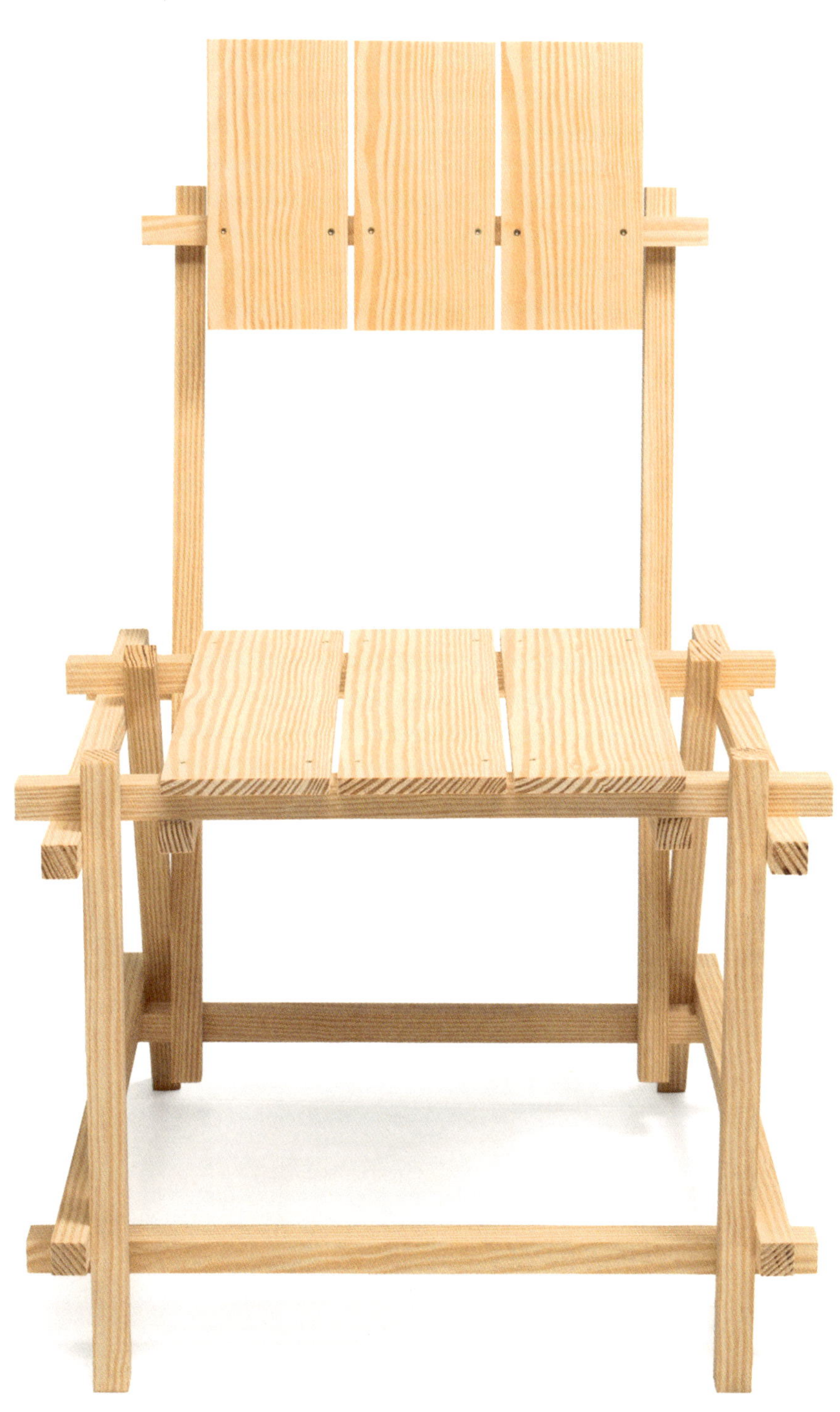

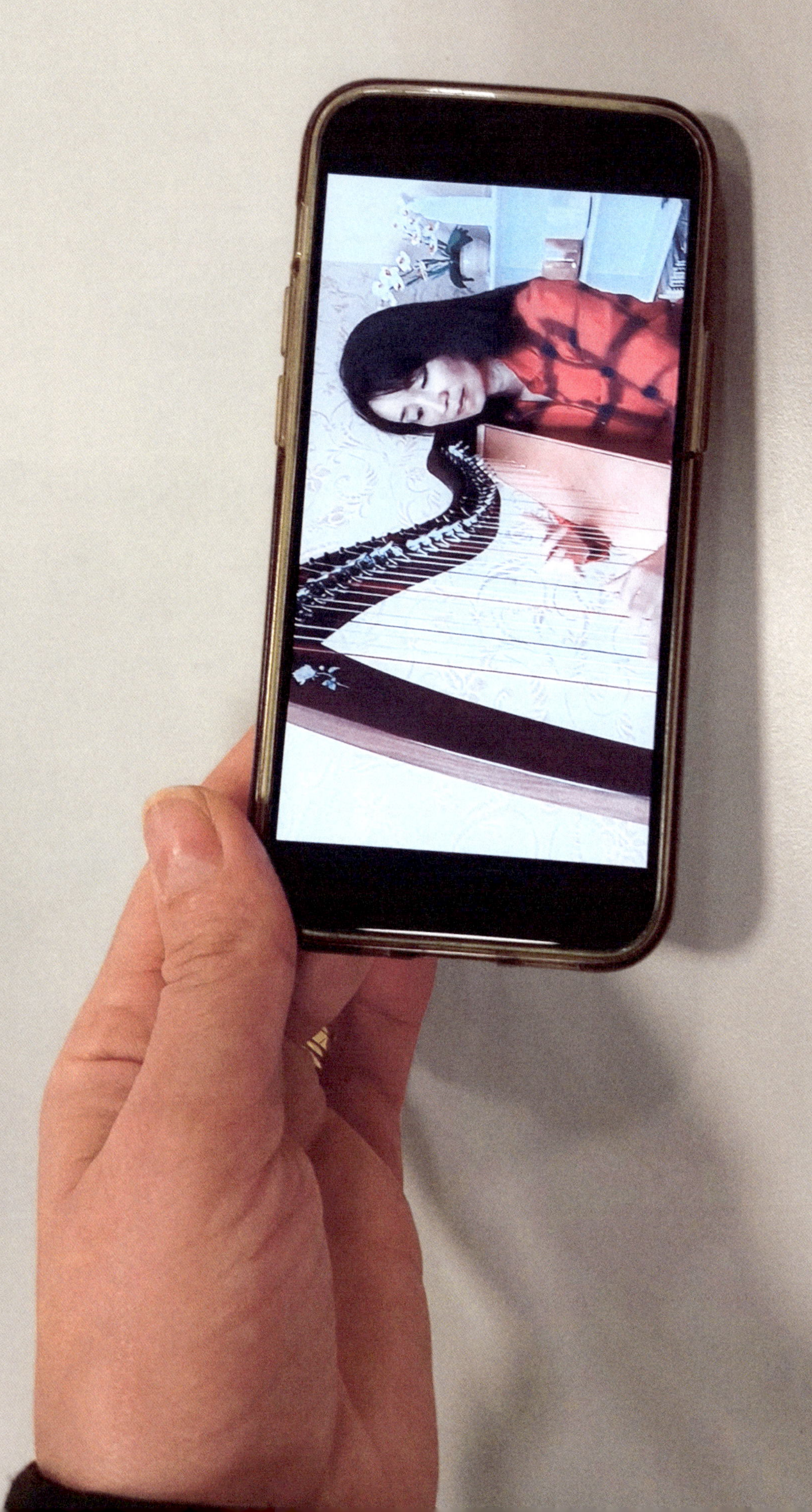

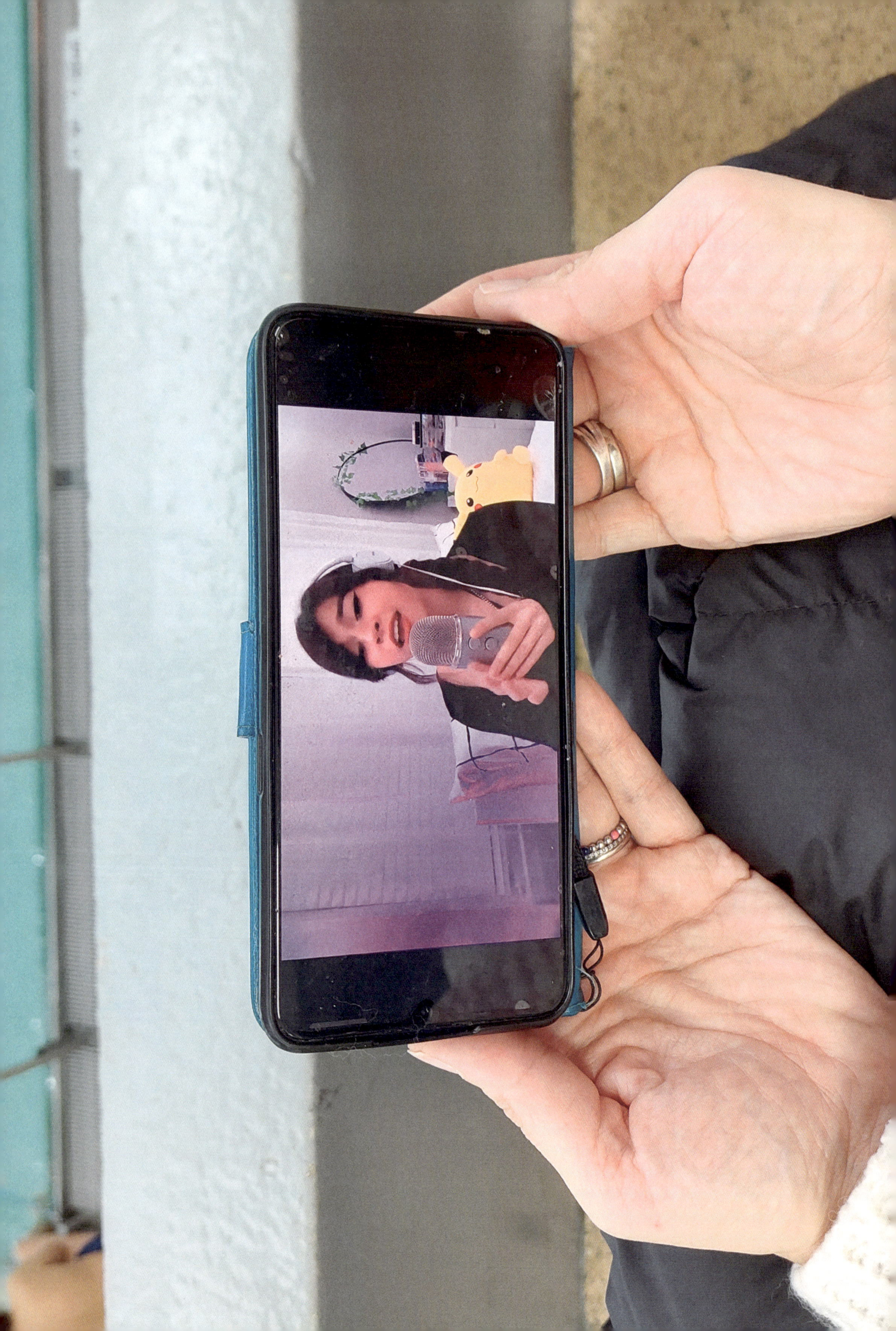

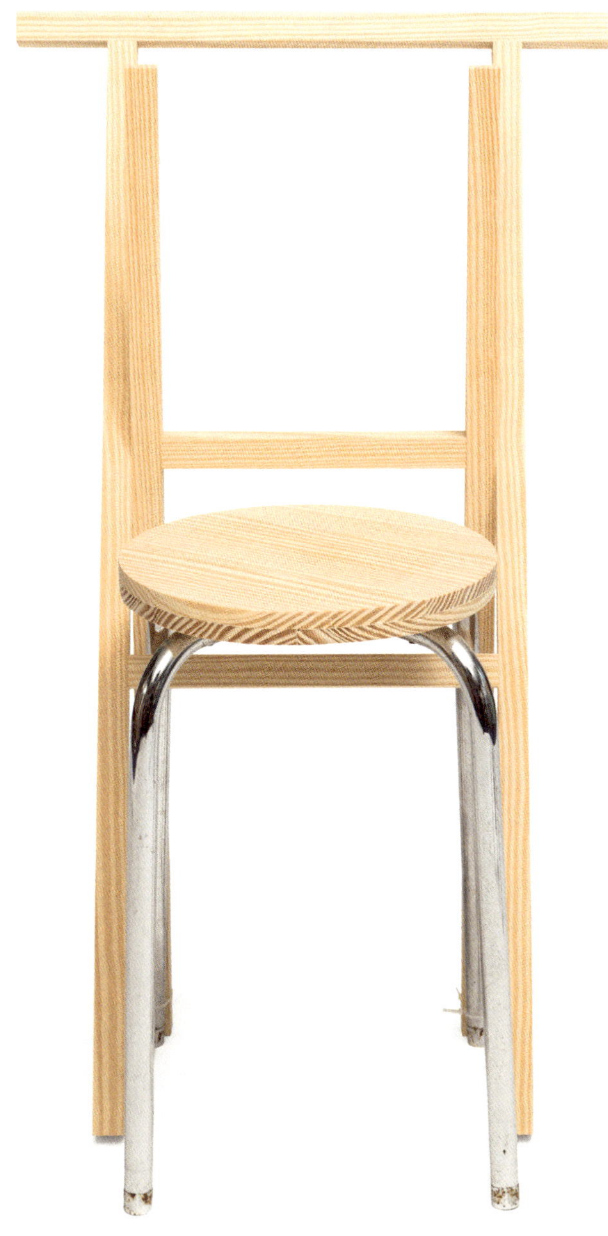

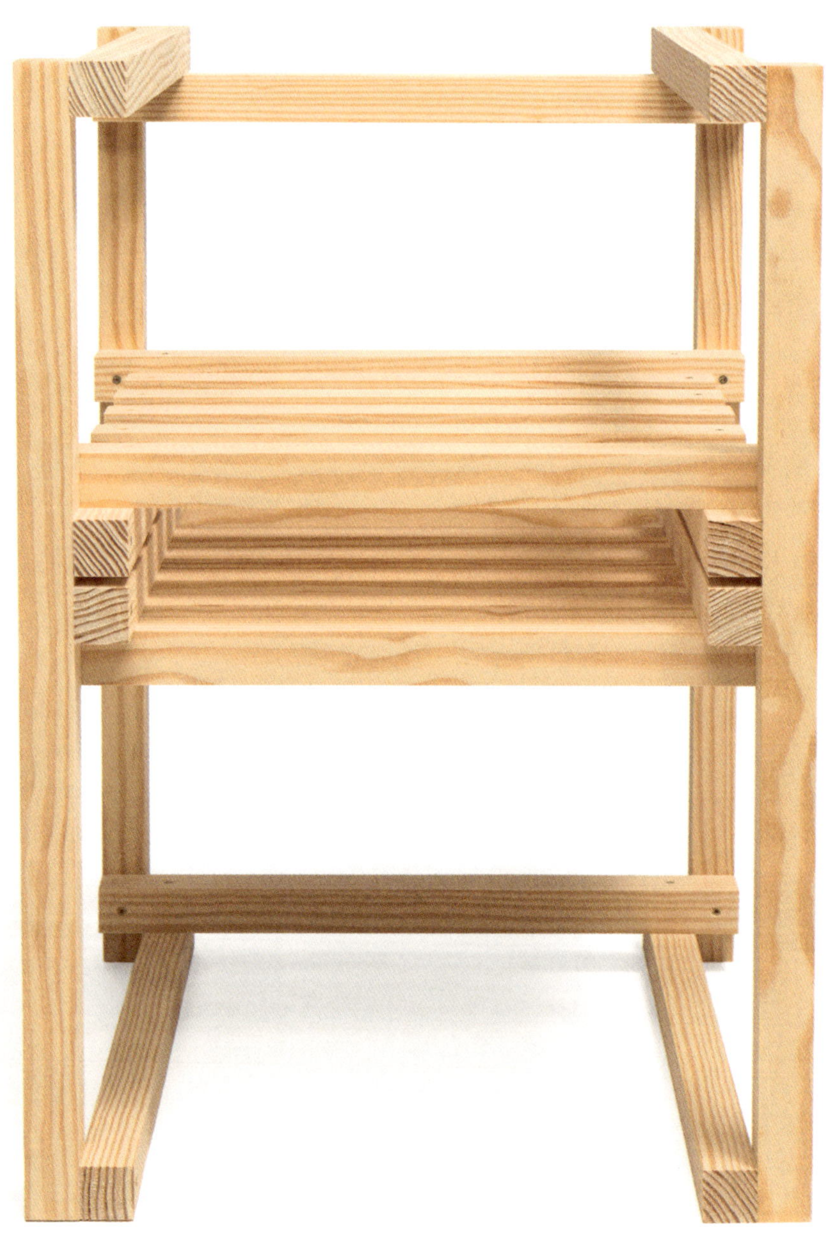

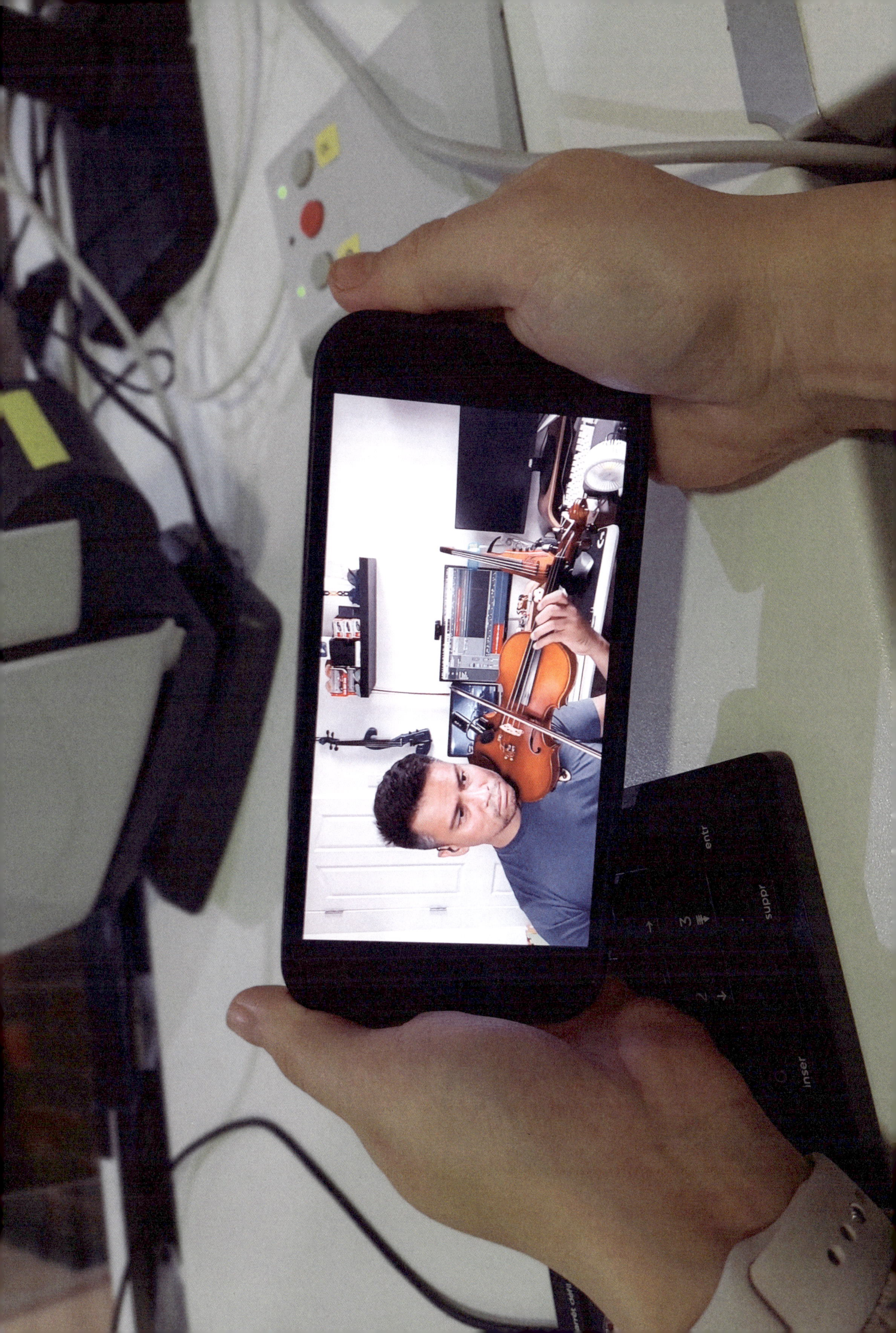

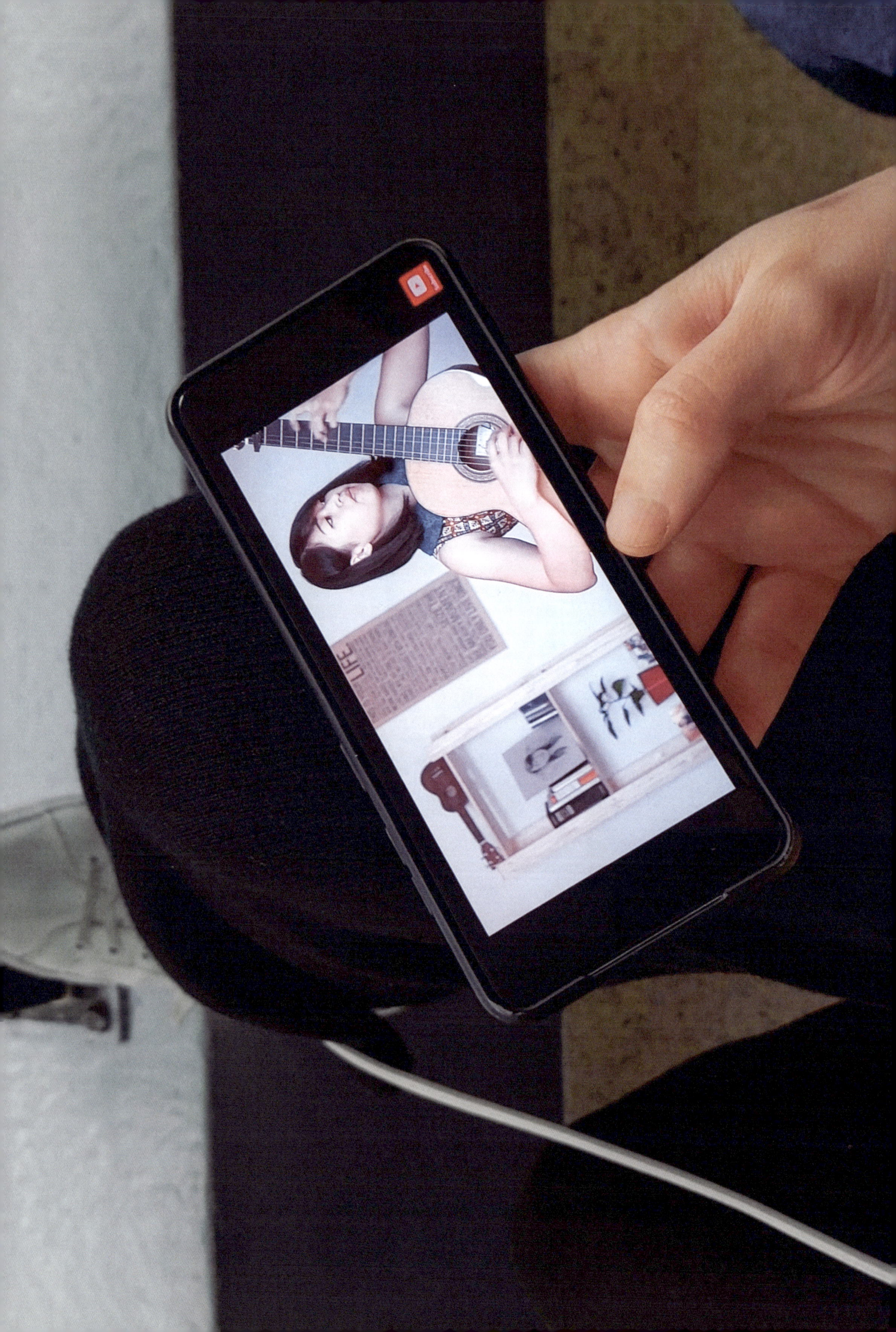

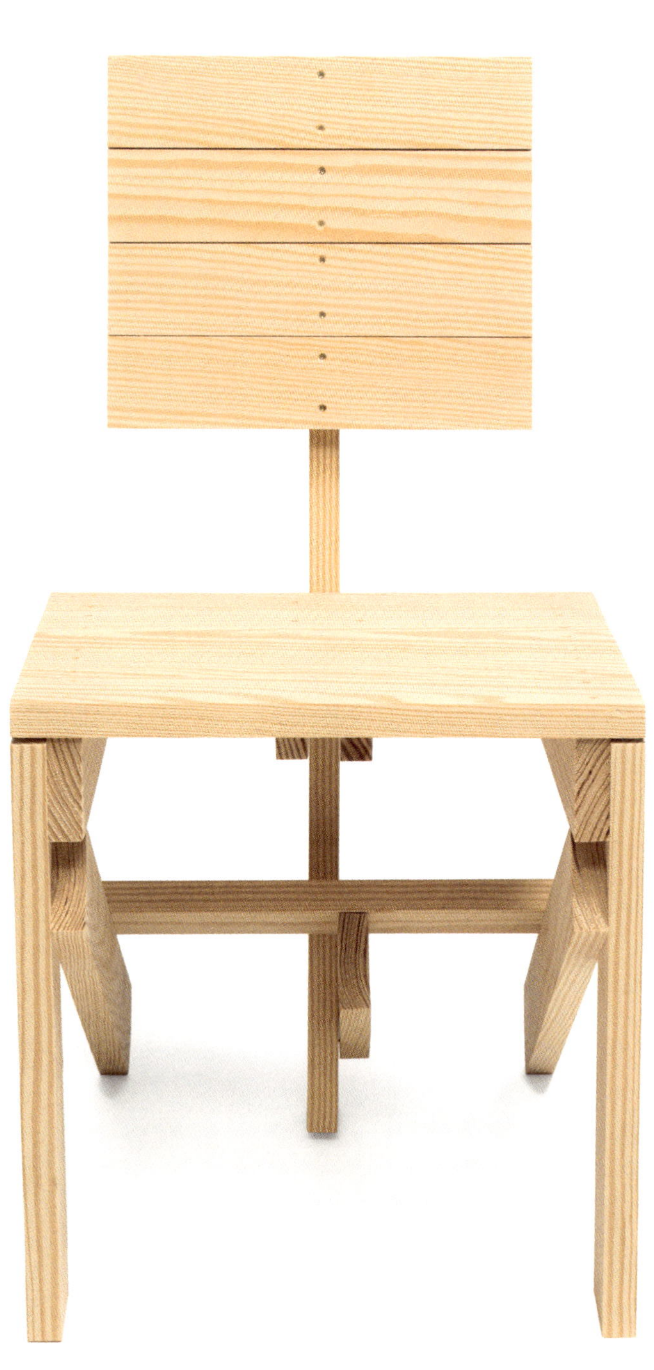

allegro

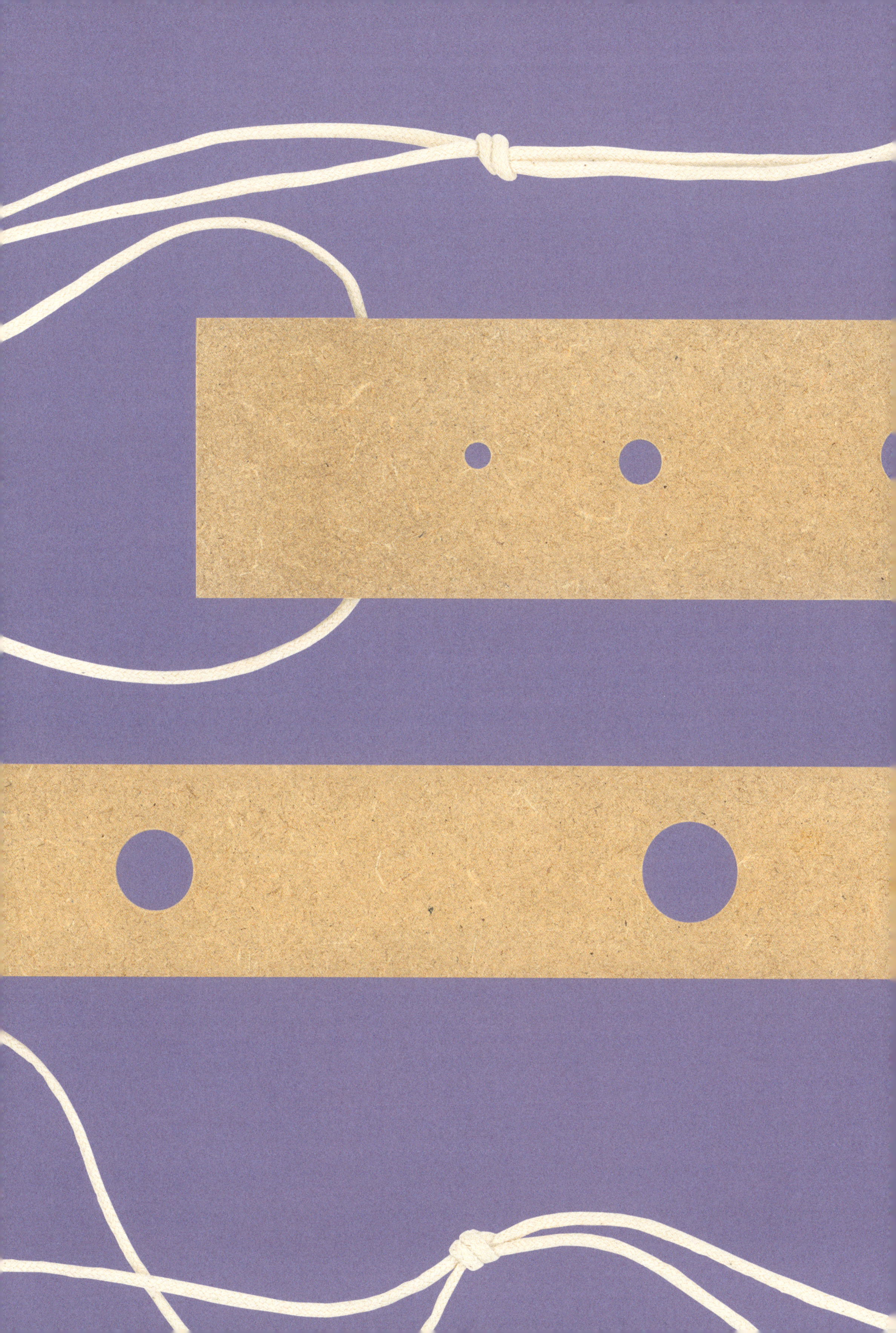

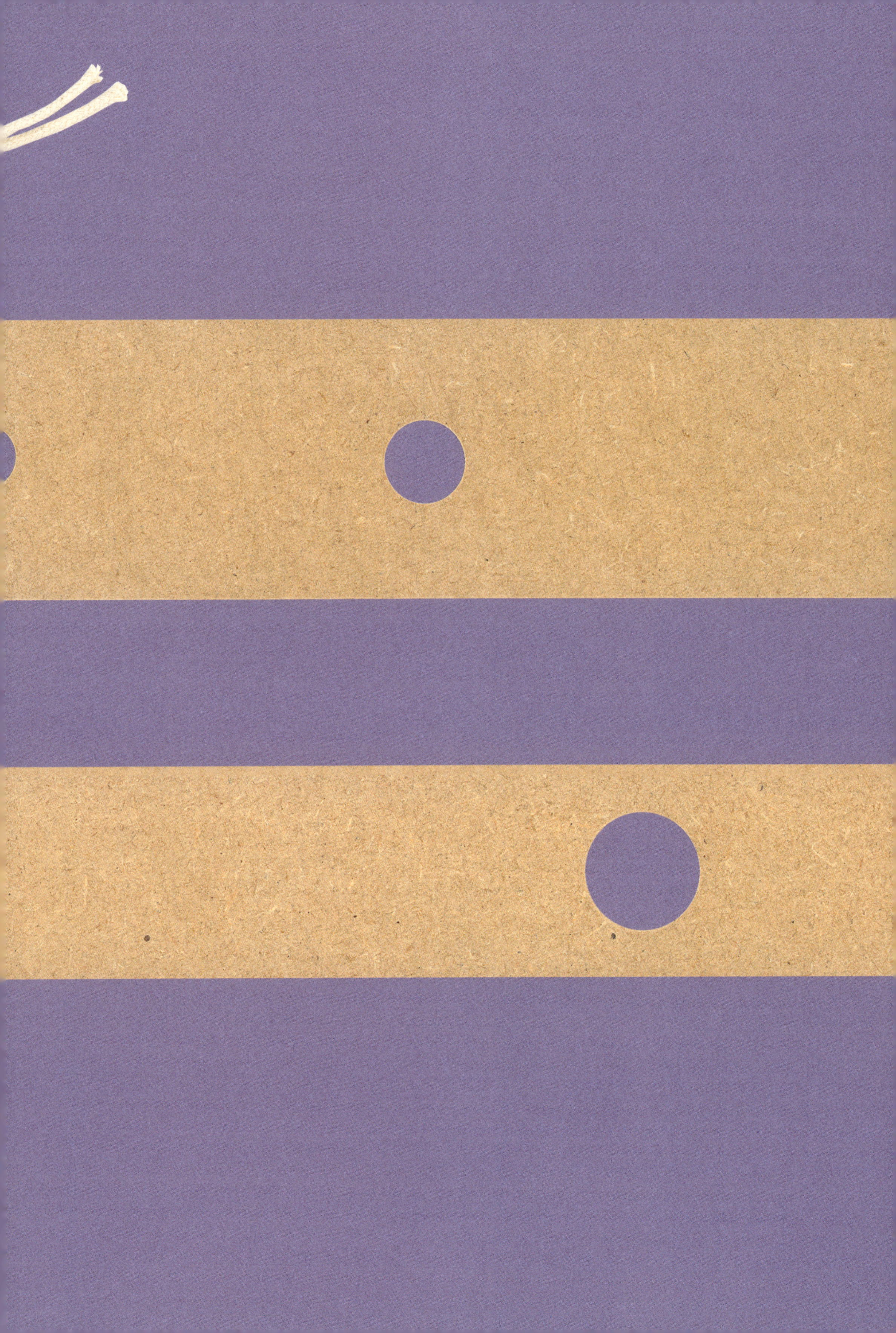

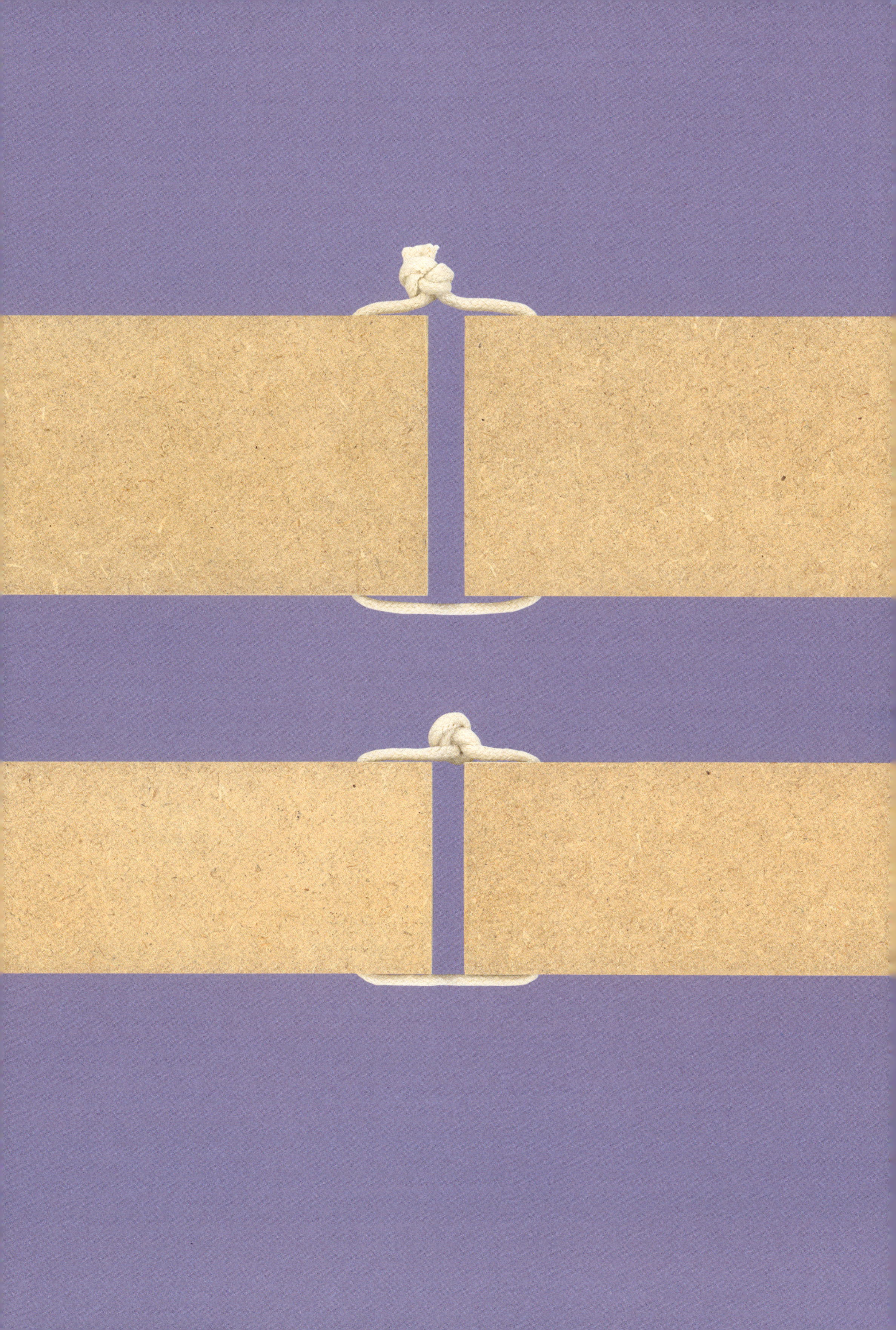

crescendo

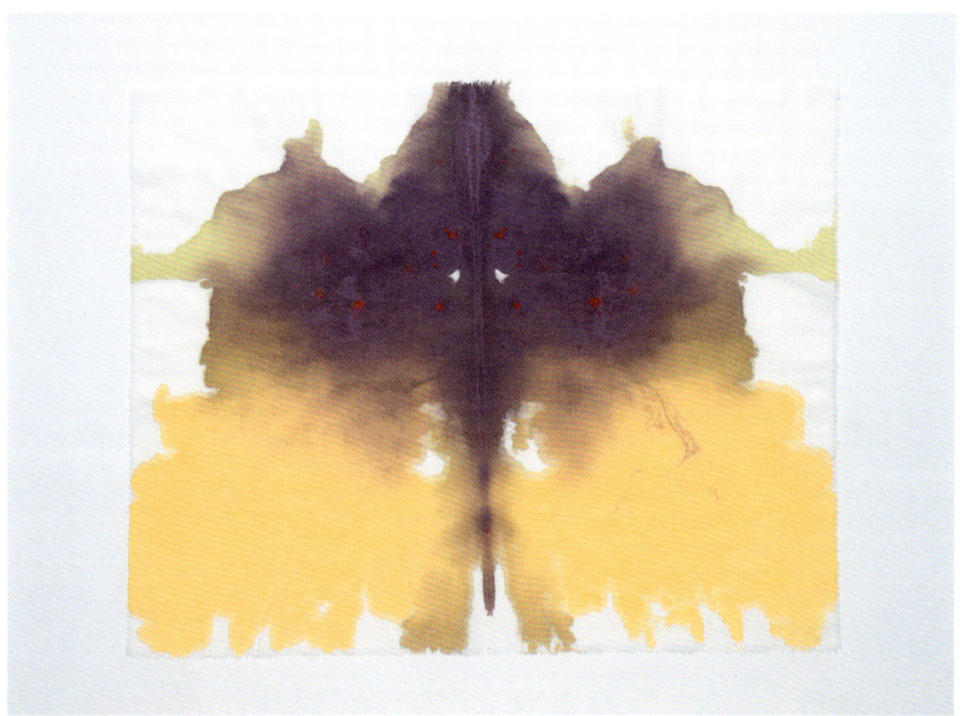

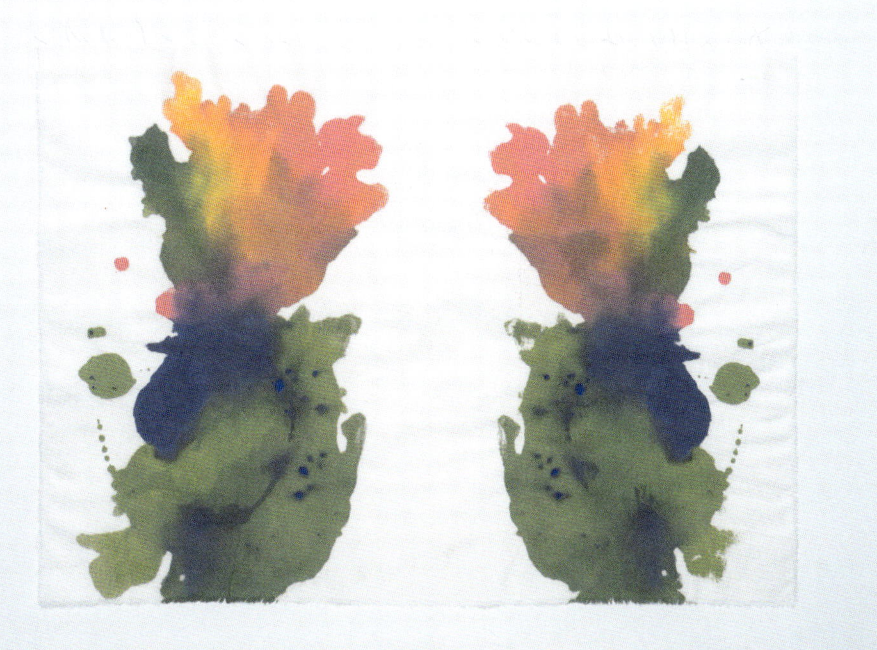

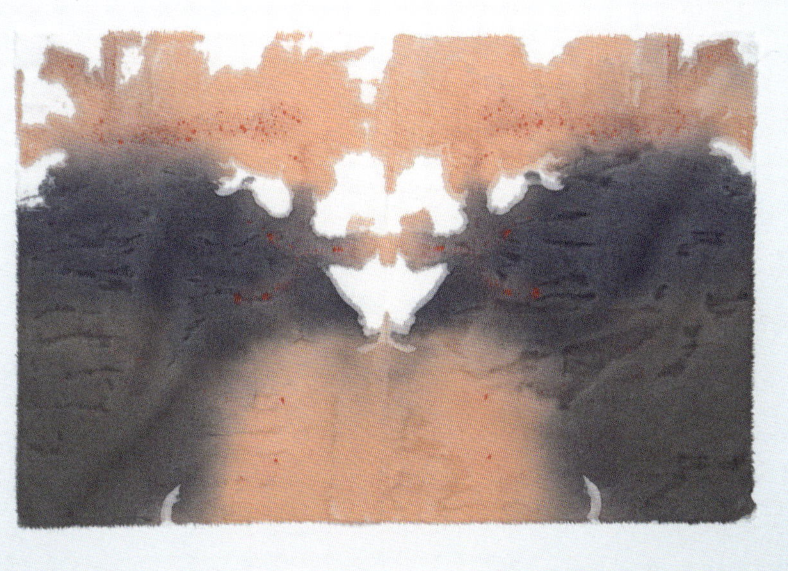

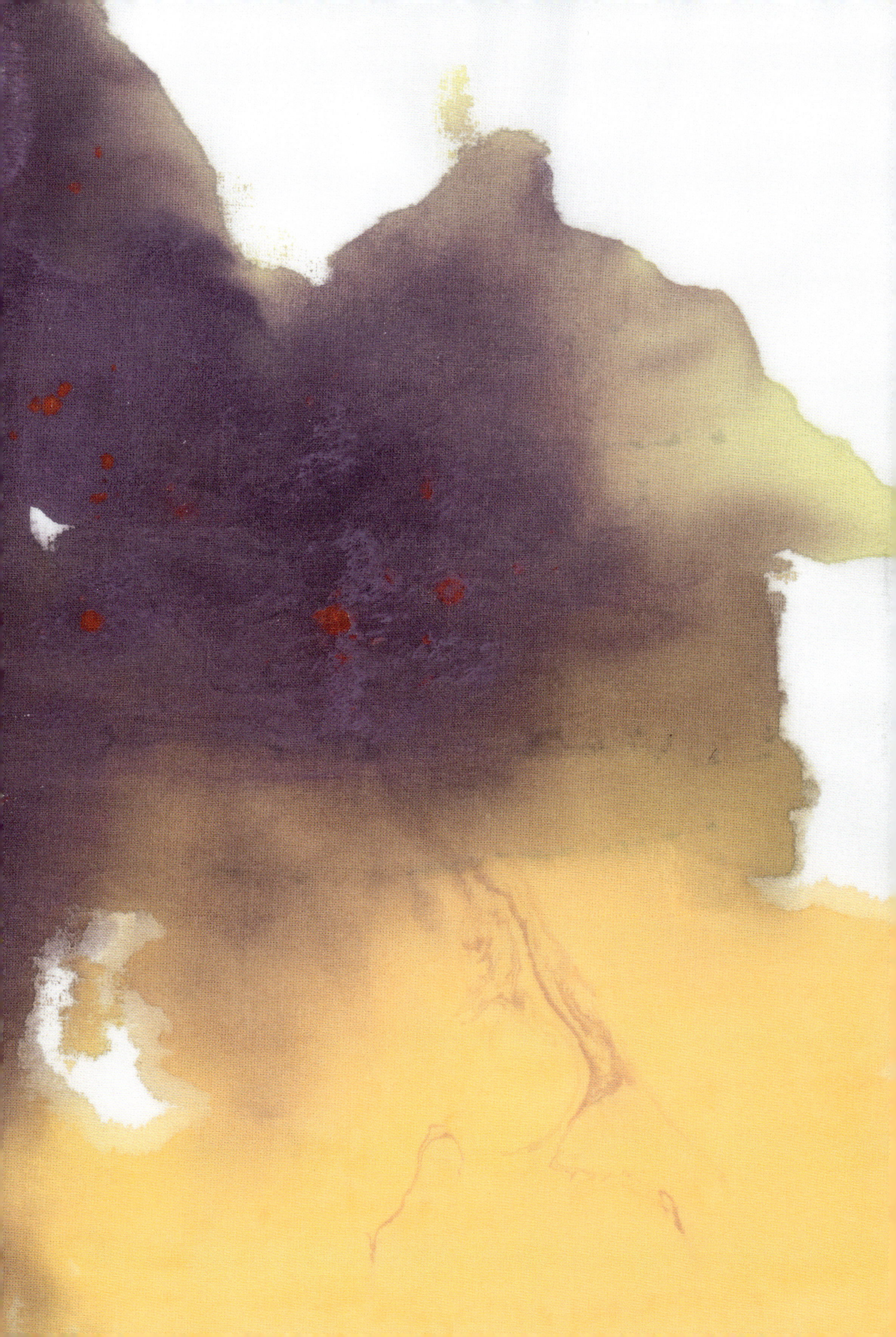

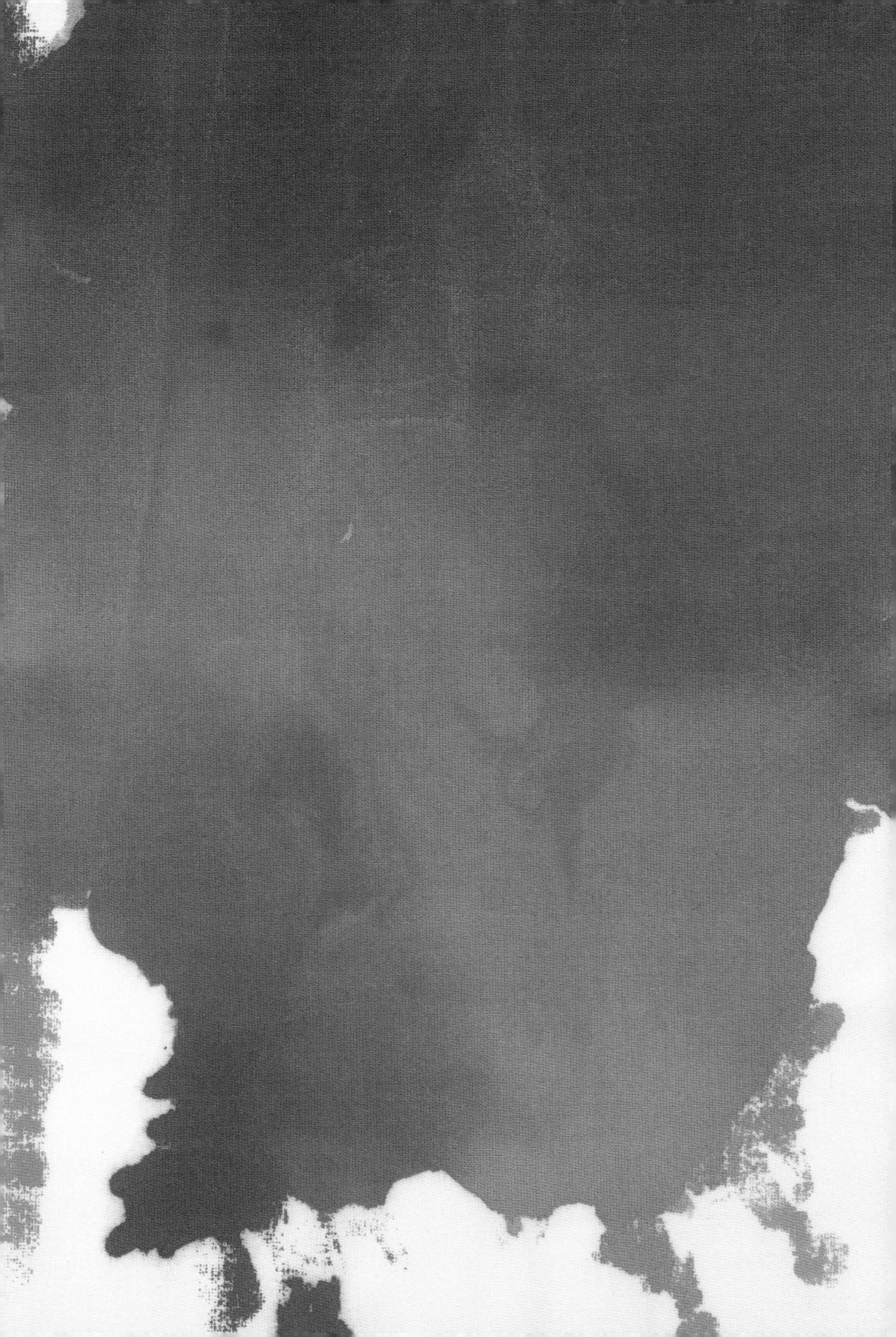

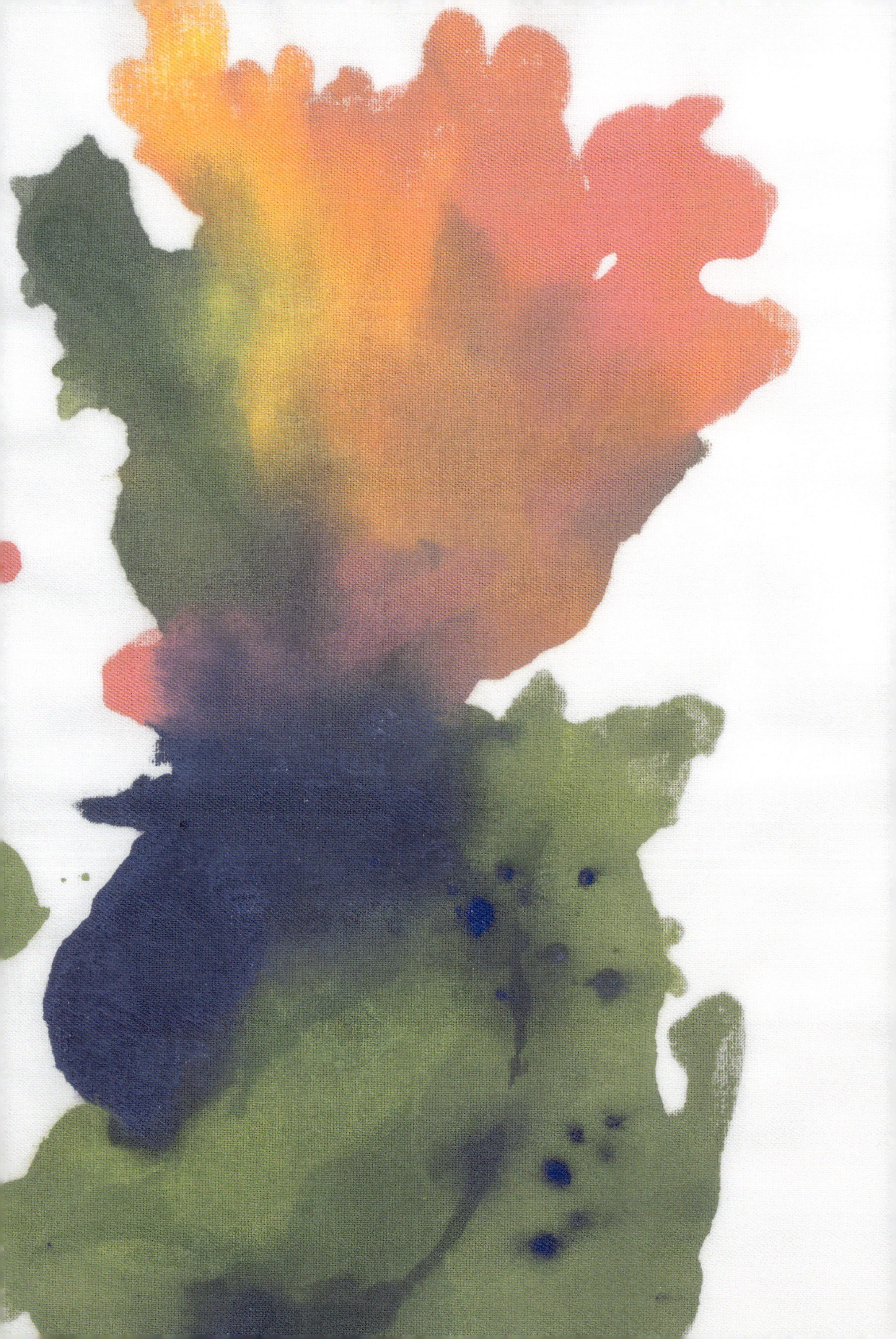

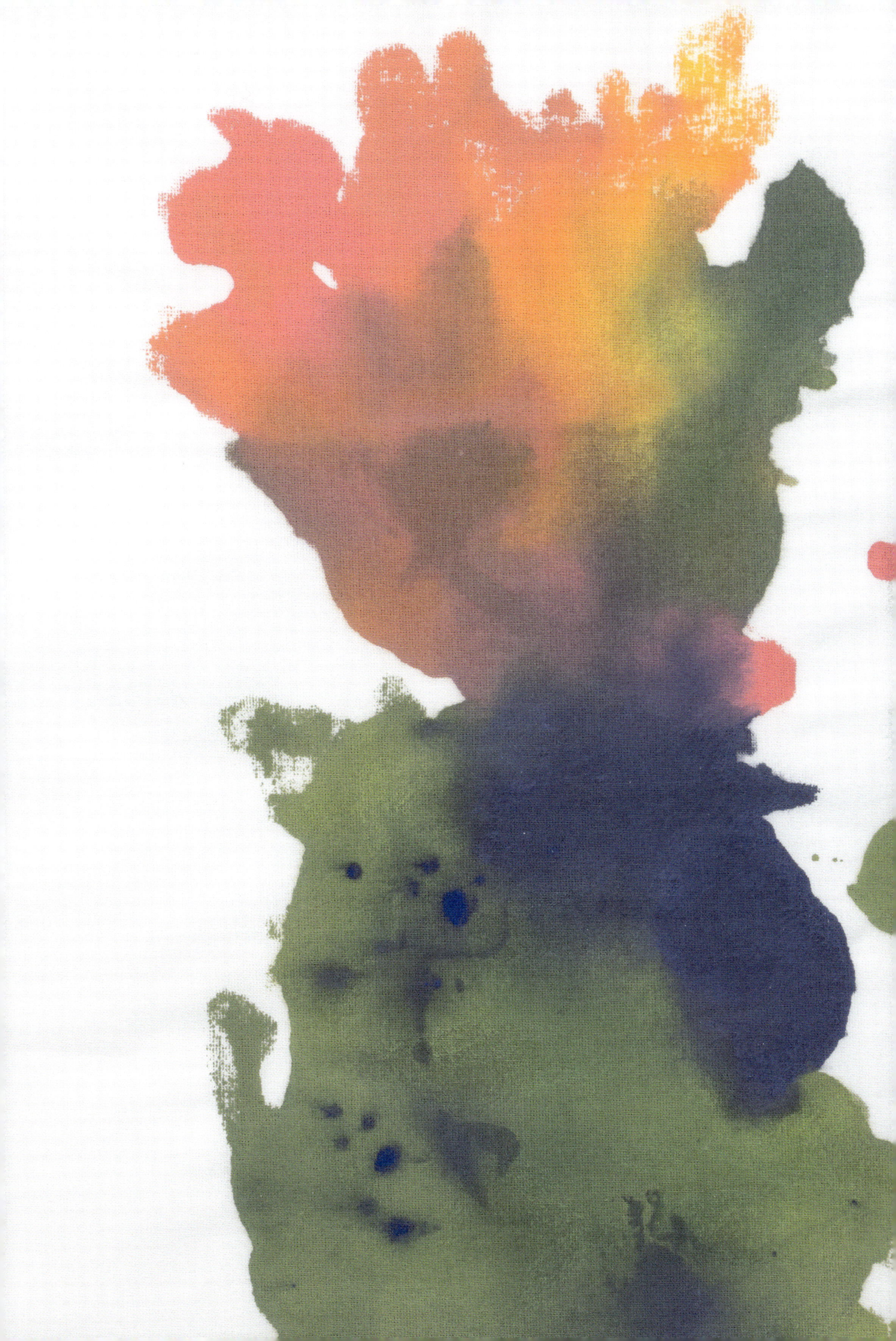

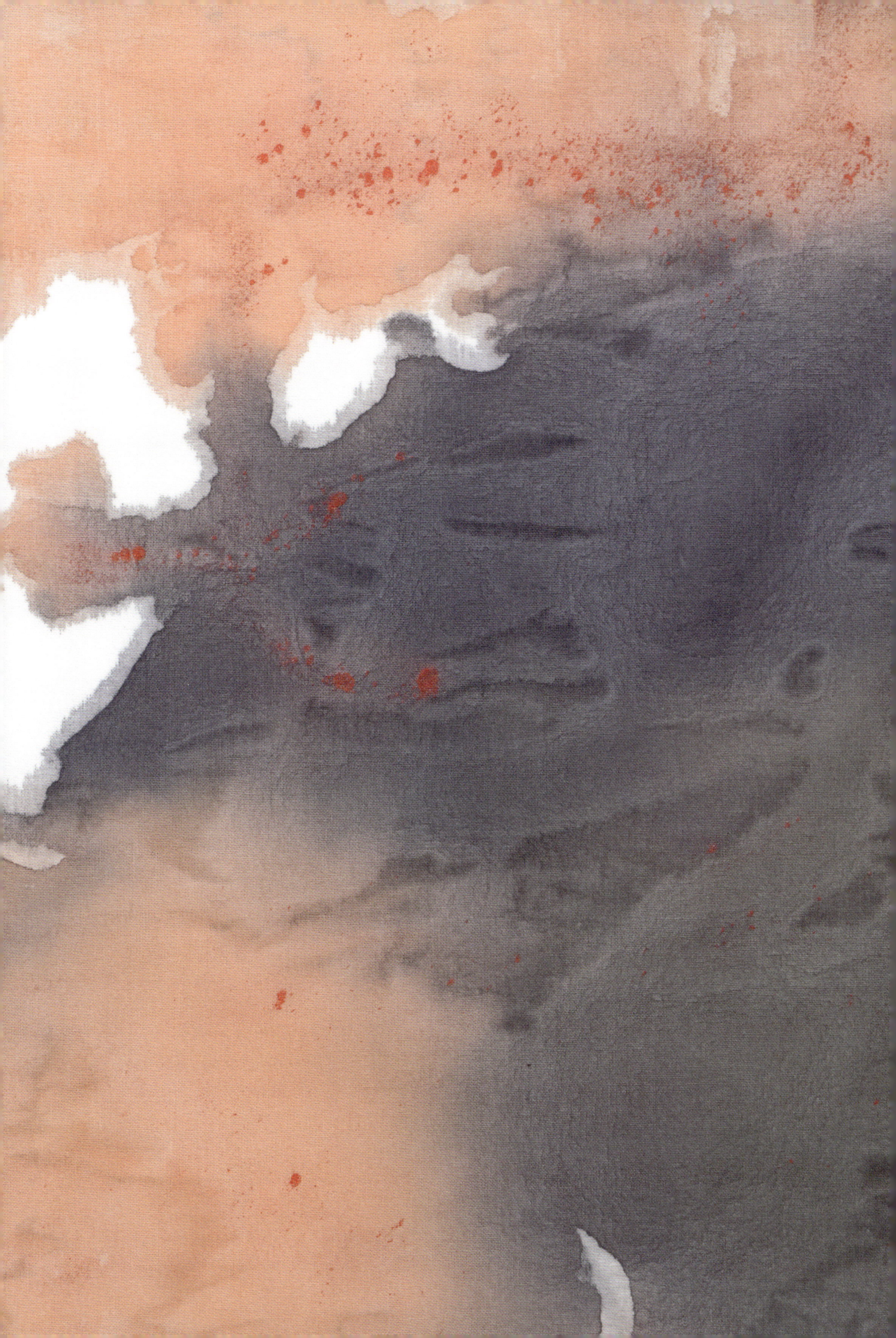

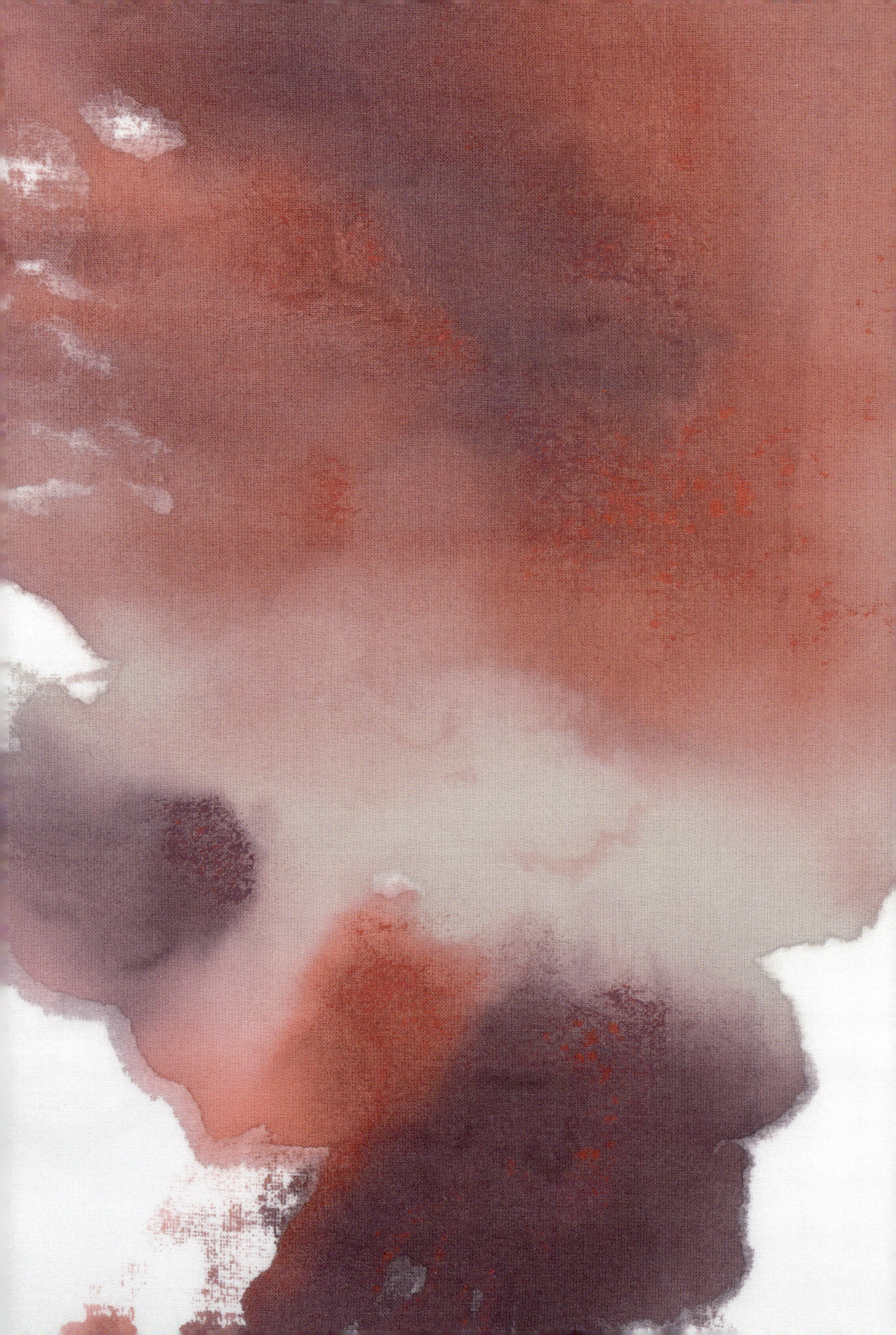

improvvisato

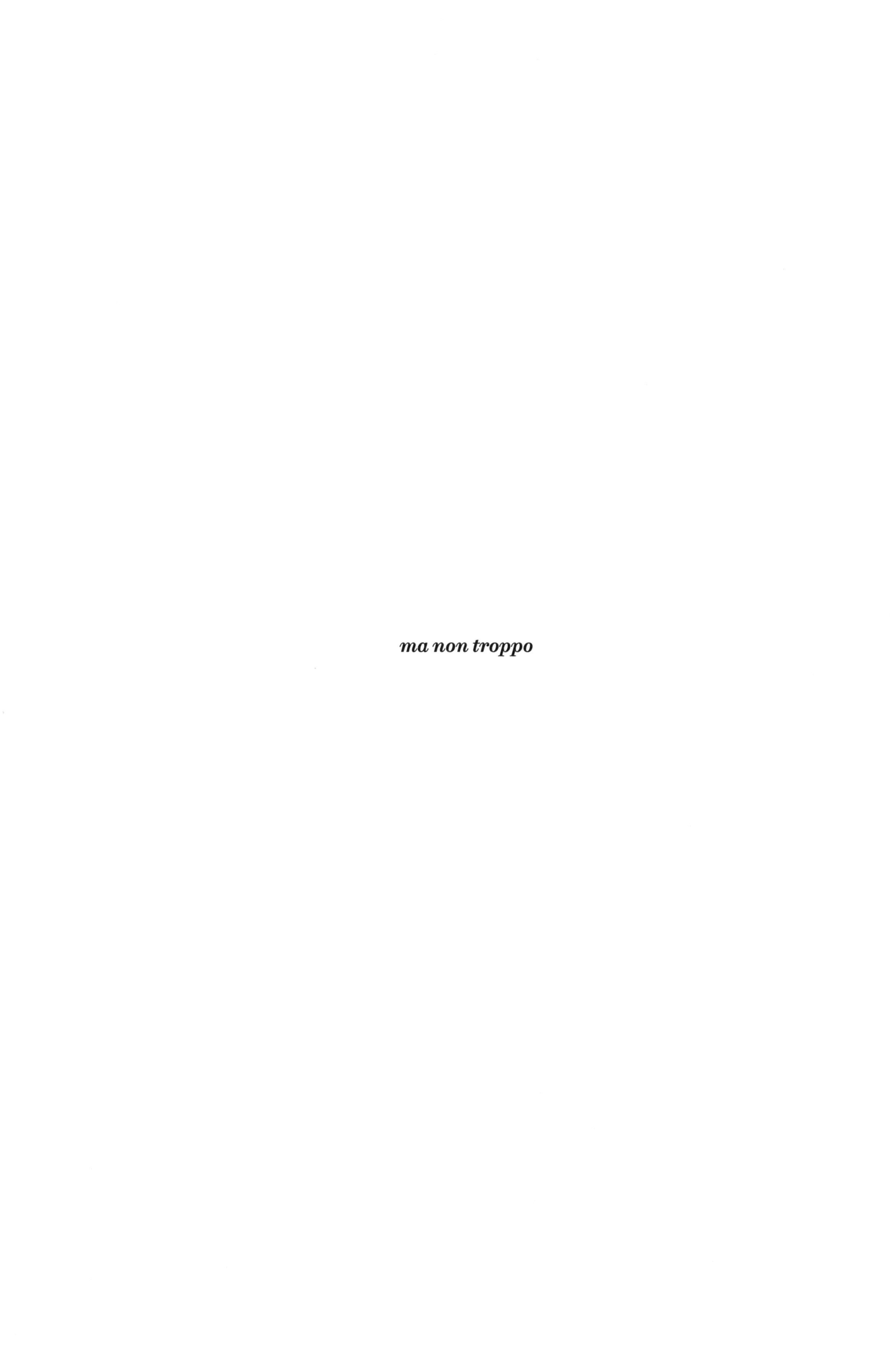

ma non troppo

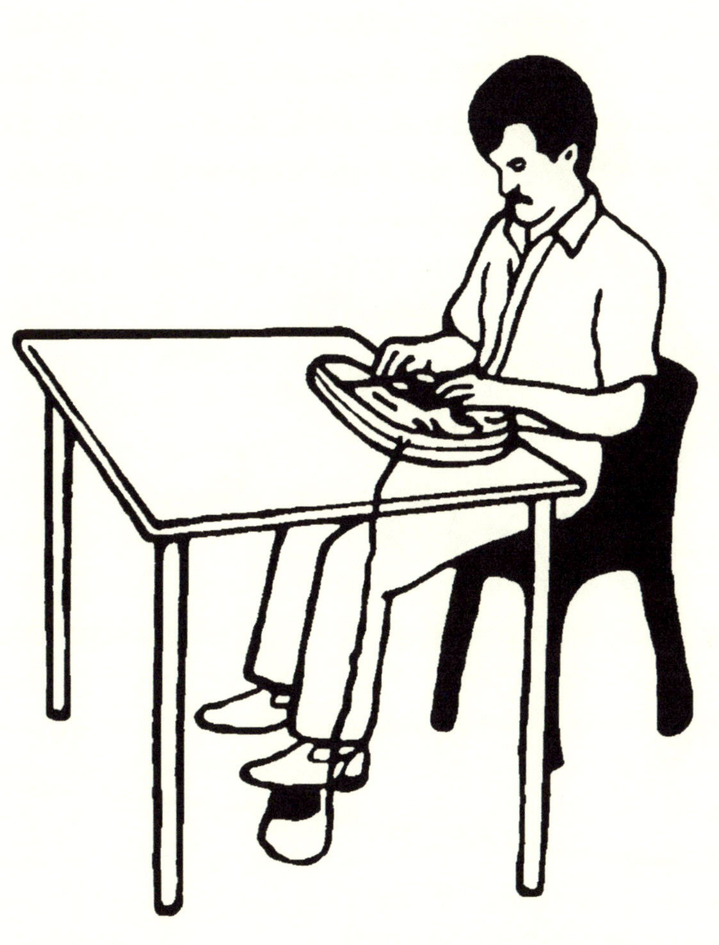

Primo Gennaio	Dodici Febbraio	Venticinque Marzo
Due Gennaio	Tredici Febbraio	Ventisei Marzo
Tre Gennaio	Quattordici Febbraio	Ventisette Marzo
Quattro Gennaio	Quindici Febbraio	Ventotto Marzo
Cinque Gennaio	Sedici Febbraio	Ventinove Marzo
Sei Gennaio	Diciassette Febbraio	Trenta Marzo
Sette Gennaio	Diciotto Febbraio	Trentuno Marzo
Otto Gennaio	Diciannove Febbraio	Primo Aprile
Nove Gennaio	Venti Febbraio	Due Aprile
Dieci Gennaio	Ventuno Febbraio	Tre Aprile
Undici Gennaio	Ventidue Febbraio	Quattro Aprile
Dodici Gennaio	Ventitre Febbraio	Cinque Aprile
Tredici Gennaio	Ventiquattro Febbraio	Sei Aprile
Quattordici Gennaio	Venticinque Febbraio	Sette Aprile
Quindici Gennaio	Ventisei Febbraio	Otto Aprile
Sedici Gennaio	Ventisette Febbraio	Nove Aprile
Diciassette Gennaio	Ventotto Febbraio	Dieci Aprile
Diciotto Gennaio	Ventinove Febbraio	Undici Aprile
Diciannove Gennaio	Primo Marzo	Dodici Aprile
Venti Gennaio	Due Marzo	Tredici Aprile
Ventuno Gennaio	Tre Marzo	Quattordici Aprile
Ventidue Gennaio	Quattro Marzo	Quindici Aprile
Ventitre Gennaio	Cinque Marzo	Sedici Aprile
Ventiquattro Gennaio	Sei Marzo	Diciassette Aprile
Venticinque Gennaio	Sette Marzo	Diciotto Aprile
Ventisei Gennaio	Otto Marzo	Diciannove Aprile
Ventisette Gennaio	Nove Marzo	Venti Aprile
Ventotto Gennaio	Dieci Marzo	Ventuno Aprile
Ventinove Gennaio	Undici Marzo	Ventidue Aprile
Trenta Gennaio	Dodici Marzo	Ventitre Aprile
Trentuno Gennaio	Tredici Marzo	Ventiquattro Aprile
Primo Febbraio	Quattordici Marzo	Venticinque Aprile
Due Febbraio	Quindici Marzo	Ventisei Aprile
Tre Febbraio	Sedici Marzo	Ventisette Aprile
Quattro Febbraio	Diciassette Marzo	Ventotto Aprile
Cinque Febbraio	Diciotto Marzo	Ventinove Aprile
Sei Febbraio	Diciannove Marzo	Trenta Aprile
Sette Febbraio	Venti Marzo	Primo Maggio
Otto Febbraio	Ventuno Marzo	Due Maggio
Nove Febbraio	Ventidue Marzo	Tre Maggio
Dieci Febbraio	Ventitre Marzo	Quattro Maggio
Undici Febbraio	Ventiquattro Marzo	Cinque Maggio

Sei Maggio
Sette Maggio
Otto Maggio
Nove Maggio
Dieci Maggio
Undici Maggio
Dodici Maggio
Tredici Maggio
Quattordici Maggio
Quindici Maggio
Sedici Maggio
Diciassette Maggio
Diciotto Maggio
Diciannove Maggio
Venti Maggio
Ventuno Maggio
Ventidue Maggio
Ventitre Maggio
Ventiquattro Maggio
Venticinque Maggio
Ventisei Maggio
Ventisette Maggio
Ventotto Maggio
Ventinove Maggio
Trenta Maggio
Trentuno Maggio
Maggio Primo Giugno
Due Giugno
Tre Giugno
Quattro Giugno
Cinque Giugno
Sei Giugno
Sette Giugno
Otto Giugno
Nove Giugno
Dieci Giugno
Undici Giugno
Dodici Giugno
Tredici Giugno
Quattordici Giugno
Quindici Giugno
Sedici Giugno

Diciassette Giugno
Diciotto Giugno
Diciannove Giugno
Venti Giugno
Ventuno Giugno
Ventidue Giugno
Ventitre Giugno
Ventiquattro Giugno
Venticinque Giugno
Ventisei Giugno
Ventisette Giugno
Ventotto Giugno
Ventinove Giugno
Trenta Giugno
Primo Luglio
Due Luglio
Tre Luglio
Quattro Luglio
Cinque Luglio
Sei Luglio
Sette Luglio
Otto Luglio
Nove Luglio
Dieci Luglio
Undici Luglio
Dodici Luglio
Tredici Luglio
Quattordici Luglio
Quindici Luglio
Sedici Luglio
Diciassette Luglio
Diciotto Luglio
Diciannove Luglio
Venti Luglio
Ventuno Luglio
Ventidue Luglio
Ventitre Luglio
Ventiquattro Luglio
Venticinque Luglio
Ventisei Luglio
Ventisette Luglio
Ventotto Luglio

Ventinove Luglio
Trenta Luglio
Trentuno Luglio
Primo Agosto
Due Agosto
Tre Agosto
Quattro Agosto
Cinque Agosto
Sei Agosto
Sette Agosto
Otto Agosto
Nove Agosto
Dieci Agosto
Undici Agosto
Dodici Agosto
Tredici Agosto
Quattordici Agosto
Quindici Agosto
Sedici Agosto
Diciassette Agosto
Diciotto Agosto
Diciannove Agosto
Venti Agosto
Ventuno Agosto
Ventidue Agosto
Ventitre Agosto
Ventiquattro Agosto
Venticinque Agosto
Ventisei Agosto
Ventisette Agosto
Ventotto Agosto
Ventinove Agosto
Trenta Agosto
Trentuno Agosto
Primo Settembre
Due Settembre
Tre Settembre
Quattro Settembre
Cinque Settembre
Sei Settembre
Sette Settembre
Otto Settembre

Nove Settembre
Dieci Settembre
Undici Settembre
Dodici Settembre
Tredici Settembre
Quattordici Settembre
Quindici Settembre
Sedici Settembre
Diciassette Settembre
Diciotto Settembre
Diciannove Settembre
Venti Settembre
Ventuno Settembre
Ventidue Settembre
Ventitre Settembre
Ventiquattro Settembre
Venticinque Settembre
Ventisei Settembre
Ventisette Settembre
Ventotto Settembre
Ventinove Settembre
Trenta Settembre
Primo Ottobre
Due Ottobre
Tre Ottobre
Quattro Ottobre
Cinque Ottobre
Sei Ottobre
Sette Ottobre
Otto Ottobre
Nove Ottobre
Dieci Ottobre
Undici Ottobre
Dodici Ottobre
Tredici Ottobre
Quattordici Ottobre
Quindici Ottobre
Sedici Ottobre
Diciassette Ottobre
Diciotto Ottobre
Diciannove Ottobre
Venti Ottobre

Ventuno Ottobre
Ventidue Ottobre
Ventitre Ottobre
Ventiquattro Ottobre
Venticinque Ottobre
Ventisei Ottobre
Ventisette Ottobre
Ventotto Ottobre
Ventinove Ottobre
Trenta Ottobre
Trentuno Ottobre
Primo Novembre
Due Novembre
Tre Novembre
Quattro Novembre
Cinque Novembre
Sei Novembre
Sette Novembre
Otto Novembre
Nove Novembre
Dieci Novembre
Undici Novembre
Dodici Novembre
Tredici Novembre
Quattordici Novembre
Quindici Novembre
Sedici Novembre
Diciassette Novembre
Diciotto Novembre
Diciannove Novembre
Venti Novembre
Ventuno Novembre
Ventidue Novembre
Ventitre Novembre
Ventiquattro Novembre
Venticinque Novembre
Ventisei Novembre
Ventisette Novembre
Ventotto Novembre
Ventinove Novembre
Trenta Novembre
Primo Dicembre

Due Dicembre
Tre Dicembre
Quattro Dicembre
Cinque Dicembre
Sei Dicembre
Sette Dicembre
Otto Dicembre
Nove Dicembre
Dieci Dicembre
Undici Dicembre
Dodici Dicembre
Tredici Dicembre
Quattordici Dicembre
Quindici Dicembre
Sedici Dicembre
Diciassette Dicembre
Diciotto Dicembre
Diciannove Dicembre
Venti Dicembre
Ventuno Dicembre
Ventidue Dicembre
Ventitre Dicembre
Ventiquattro Dicembre
Venticinque Dicembre
Ventisei Dicembre
Ventisette Dicembre
Ventotto Dicembre
Ventinove Dicembre
Trenta Dicembre
Trentuno Dicembre

R

TEMPO   VOLUME   S

) on

WALTZ   ~~ECHO~~ BASS

+ BASS

1 M

V   T

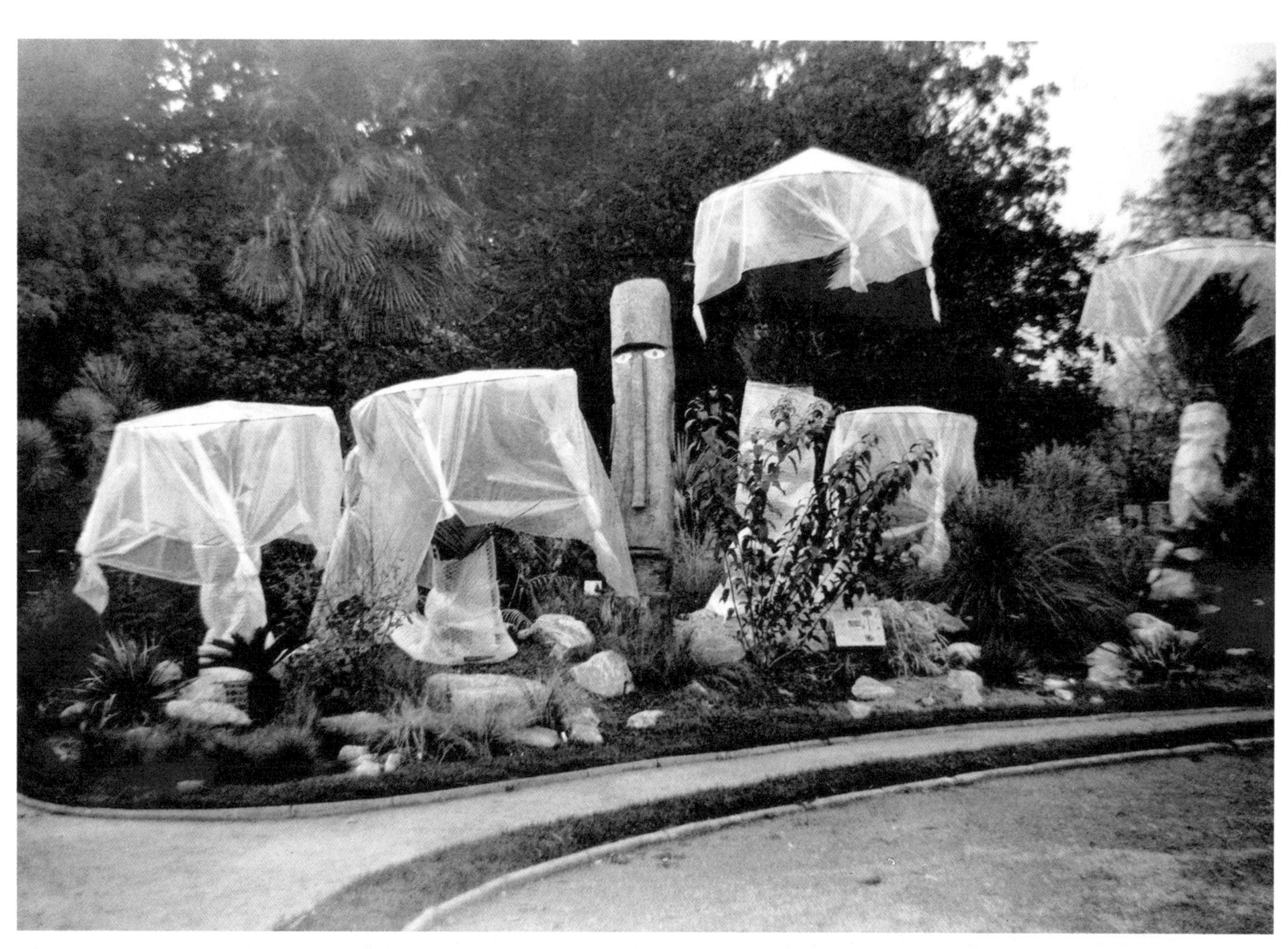

come prima

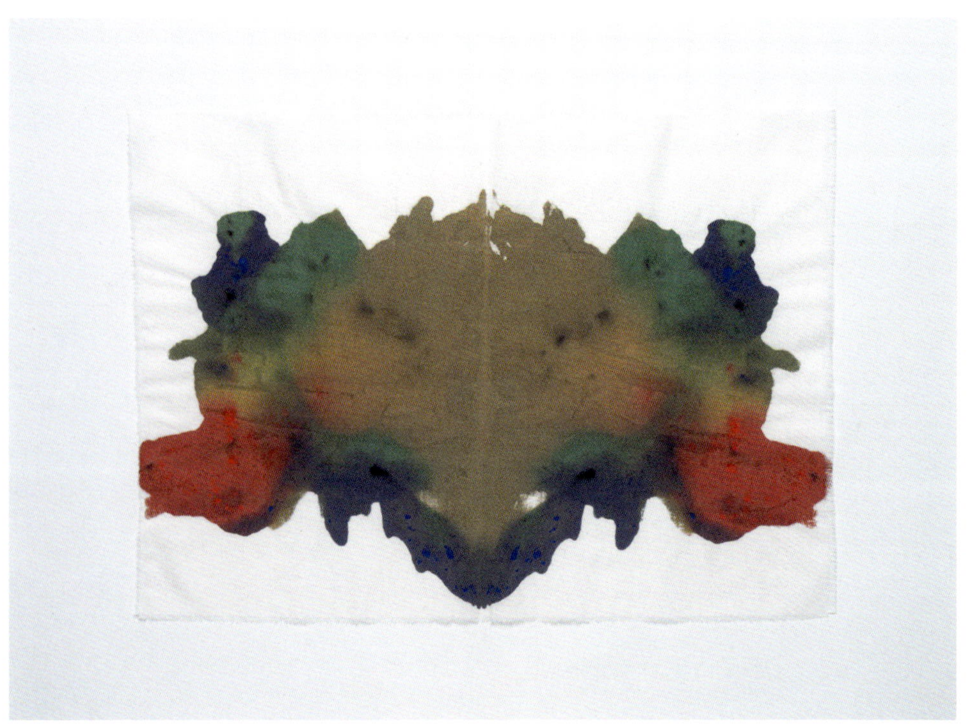

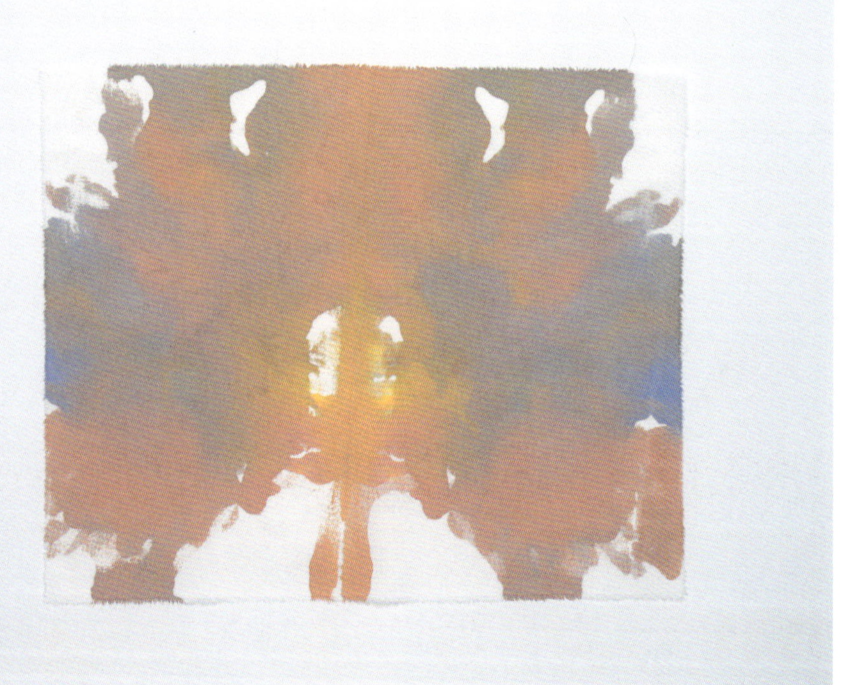

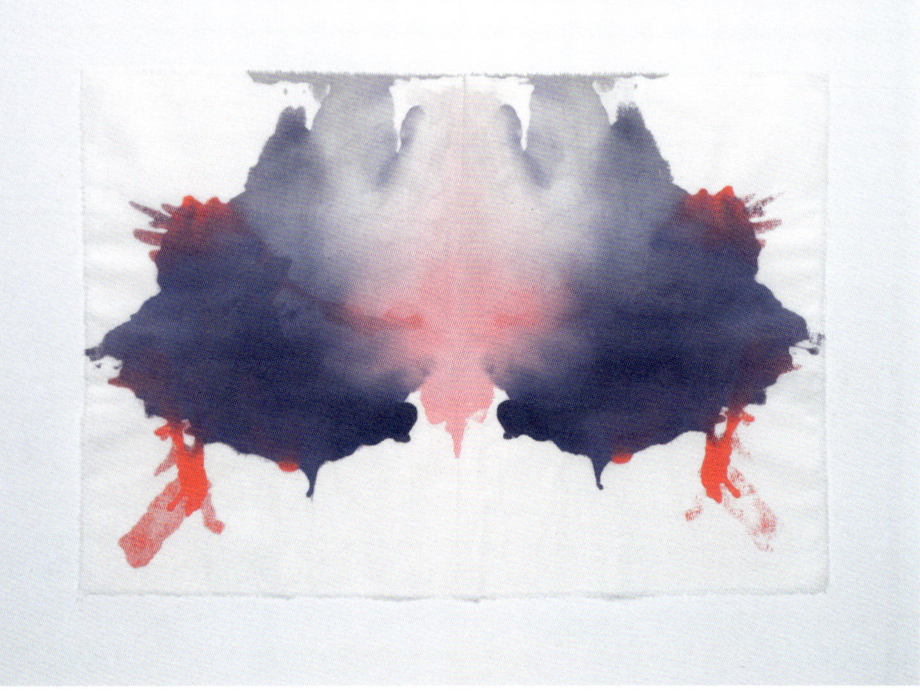

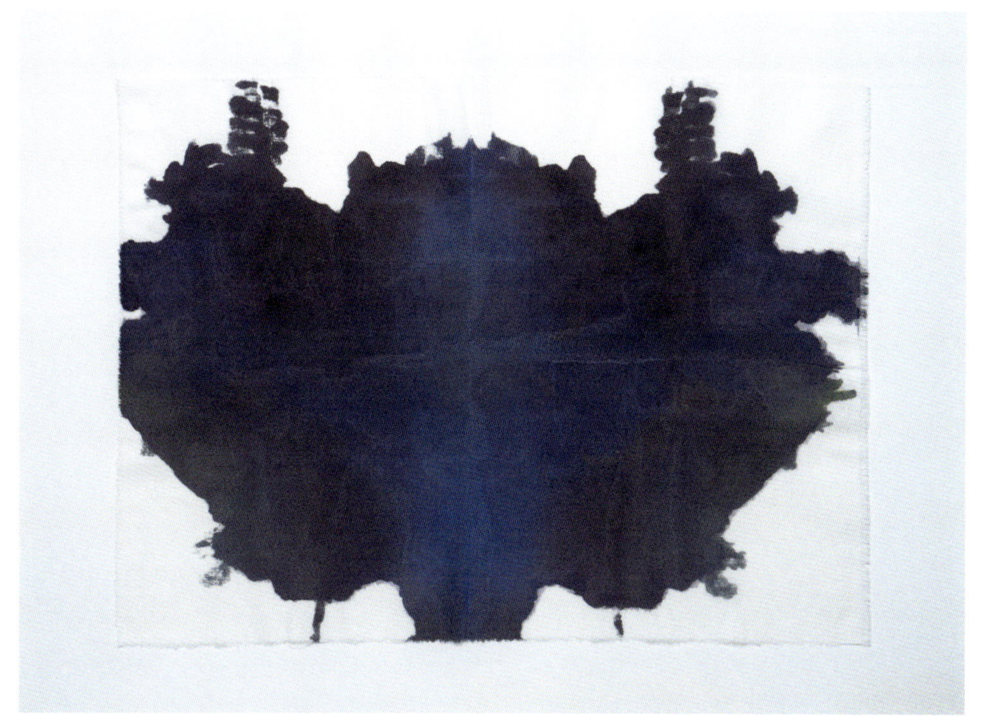

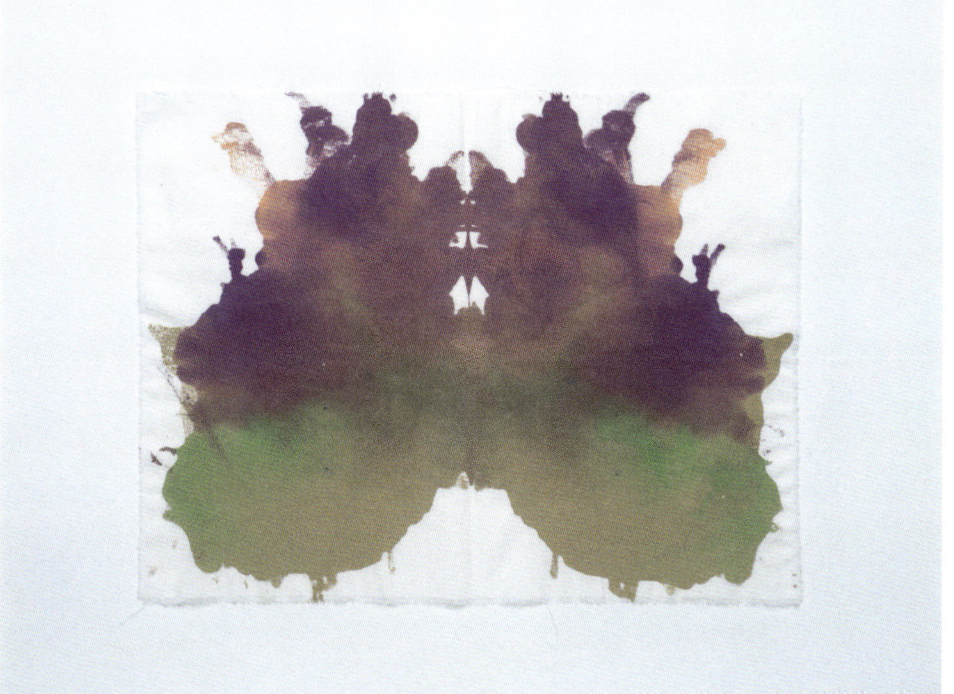

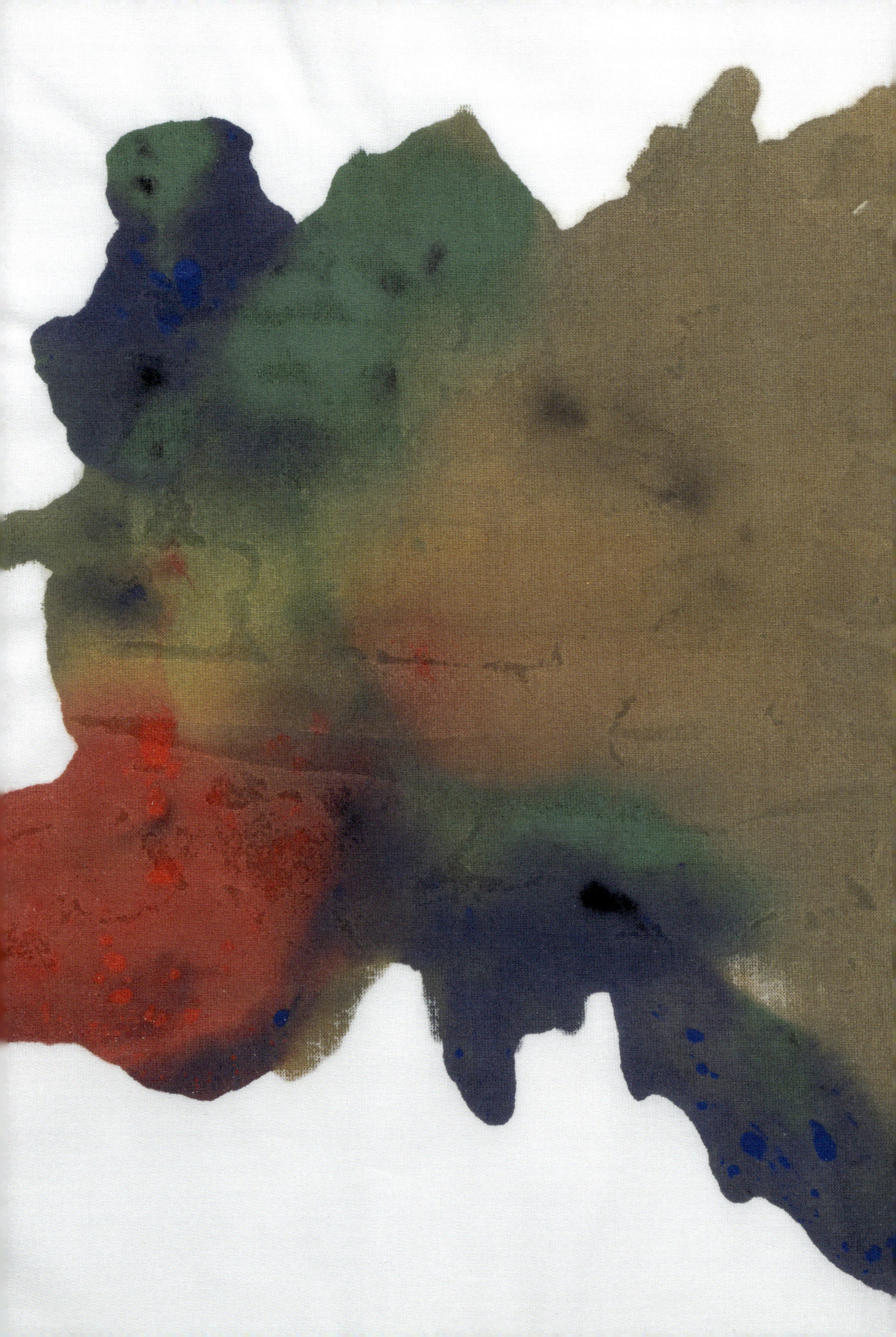

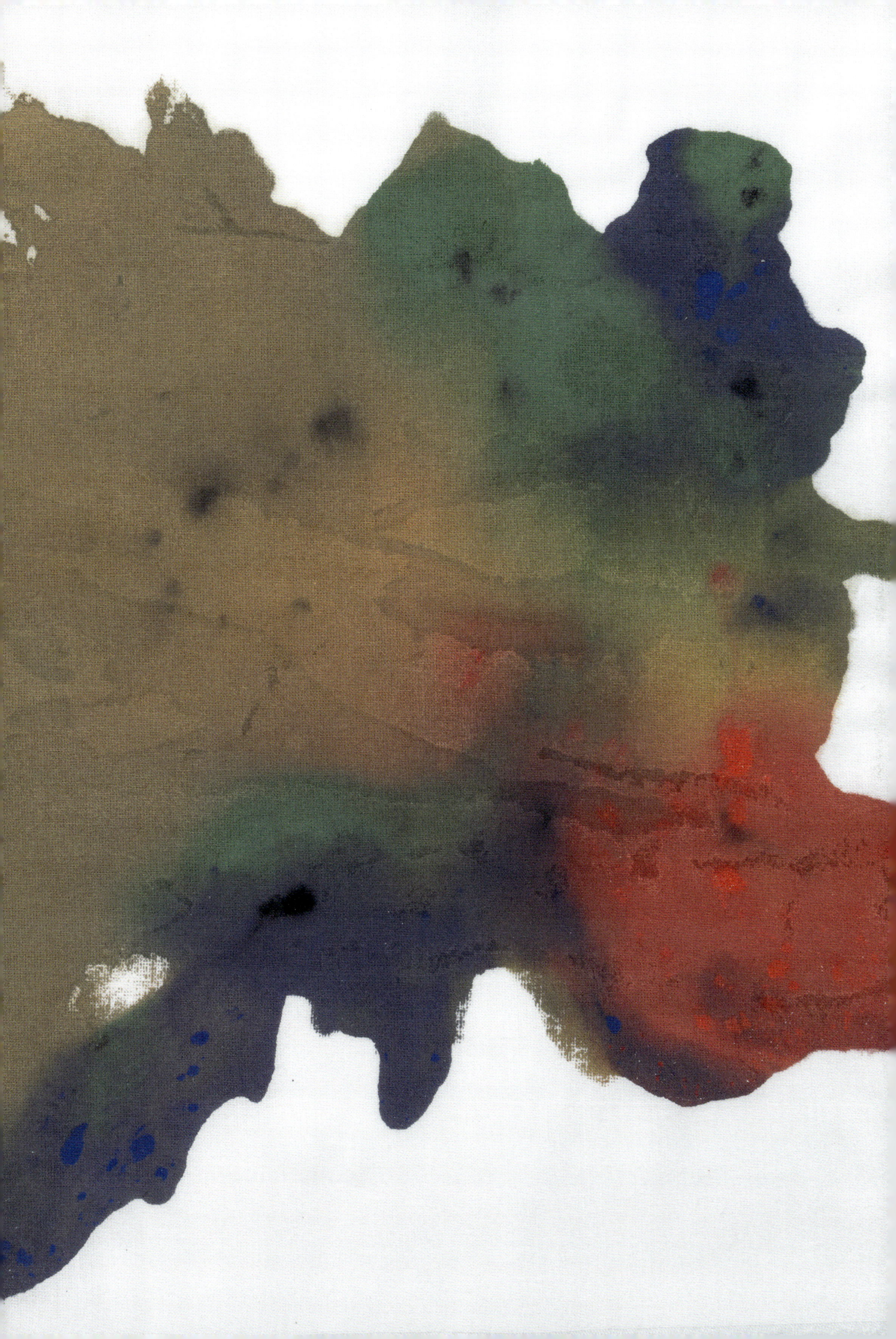

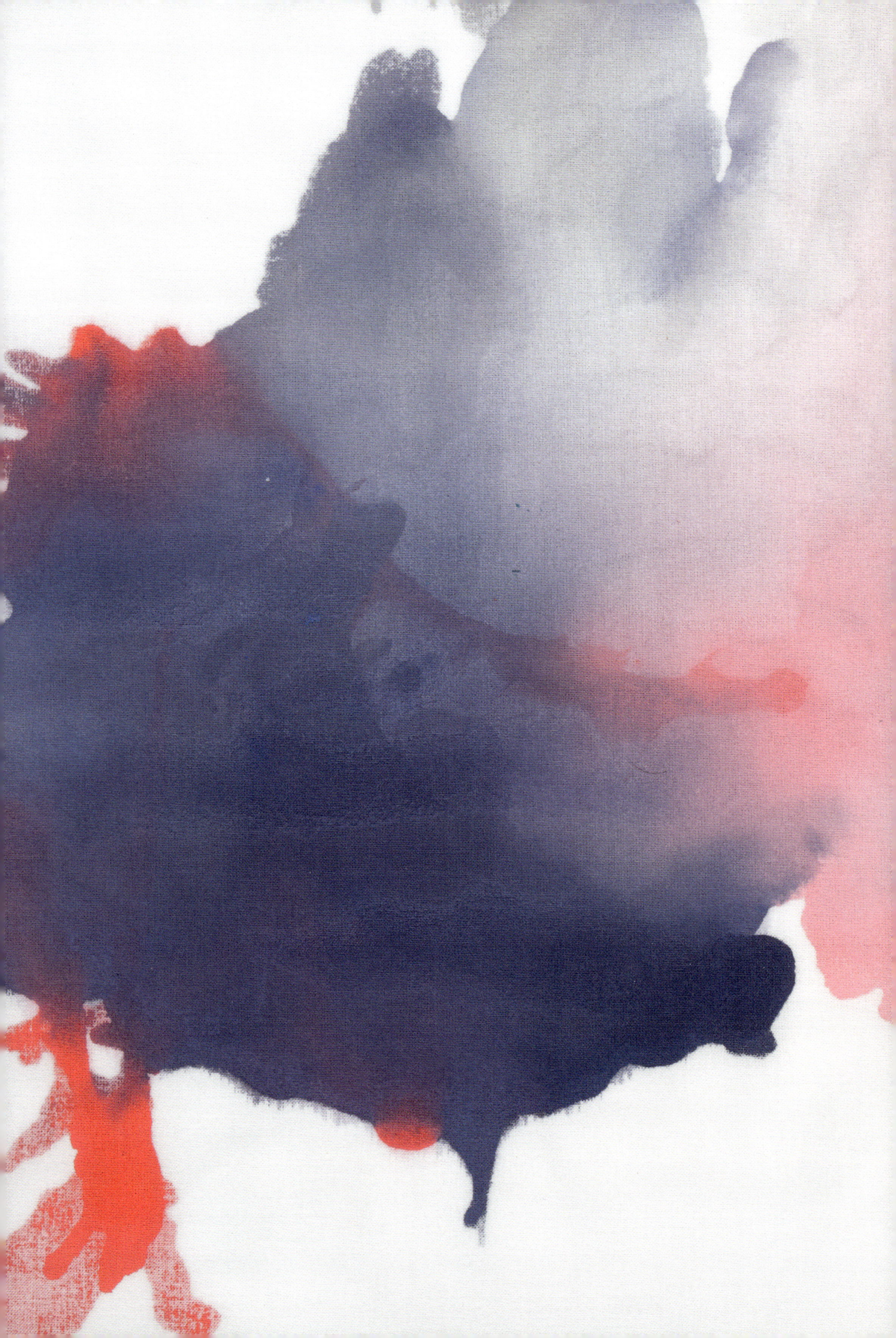

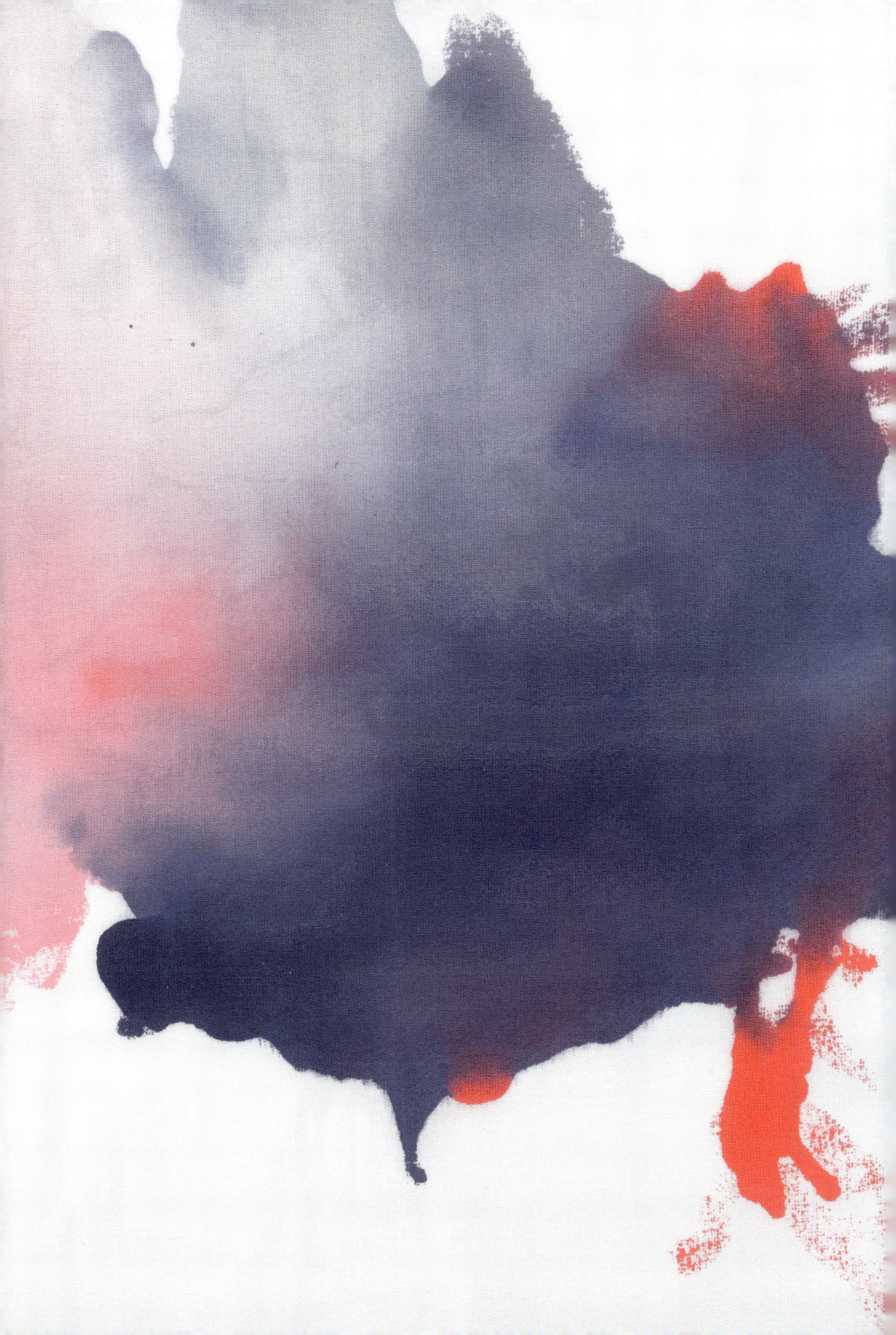

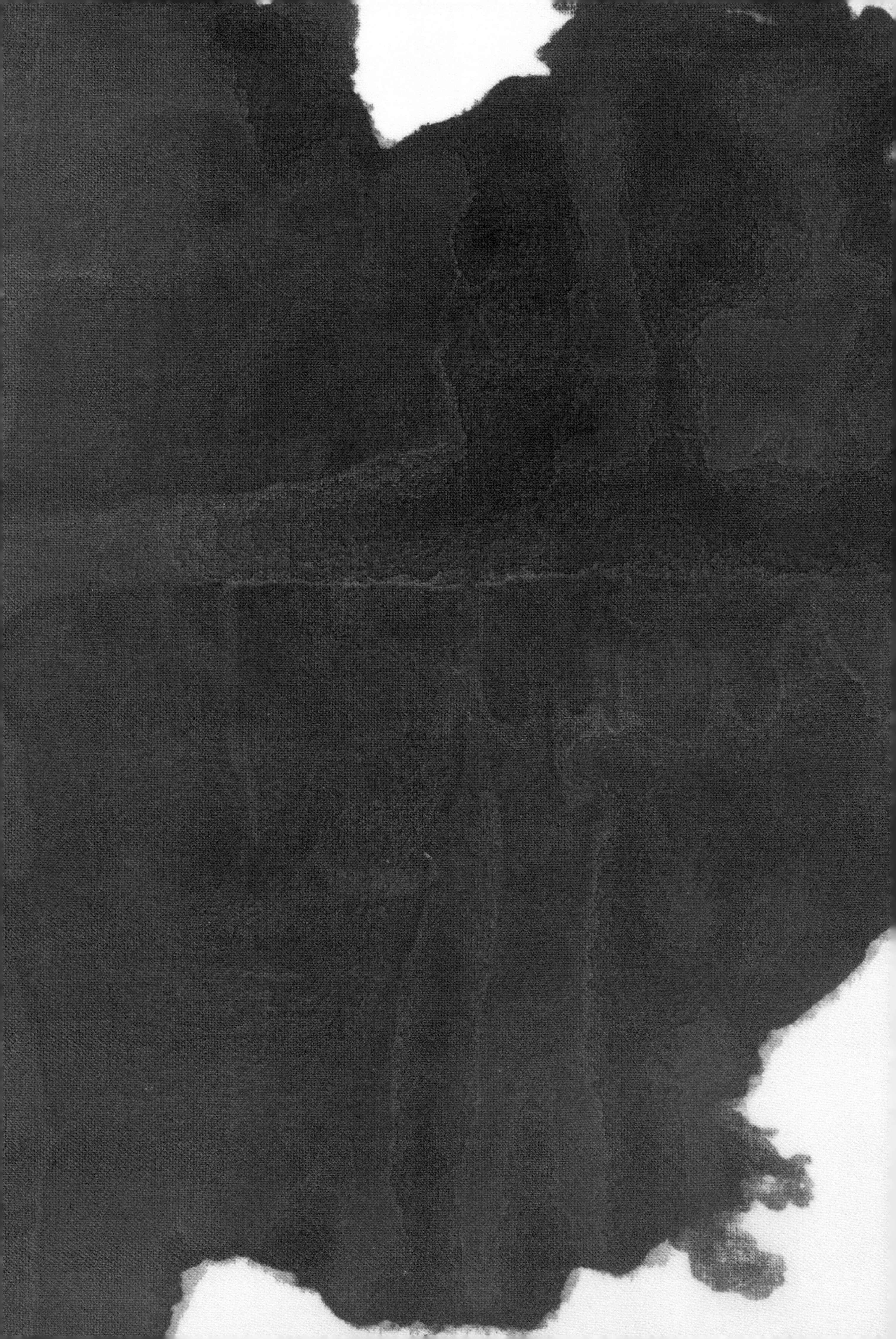

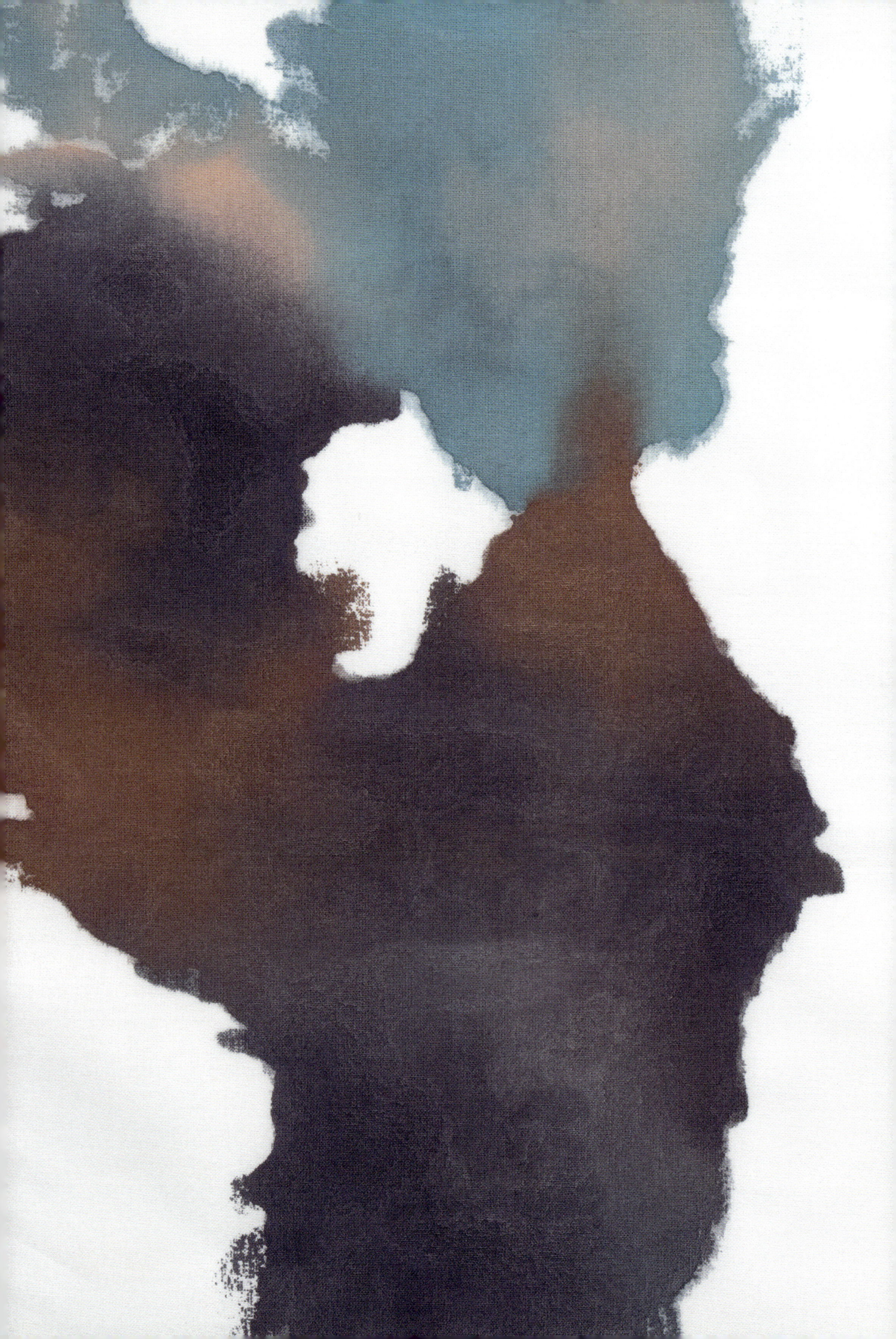

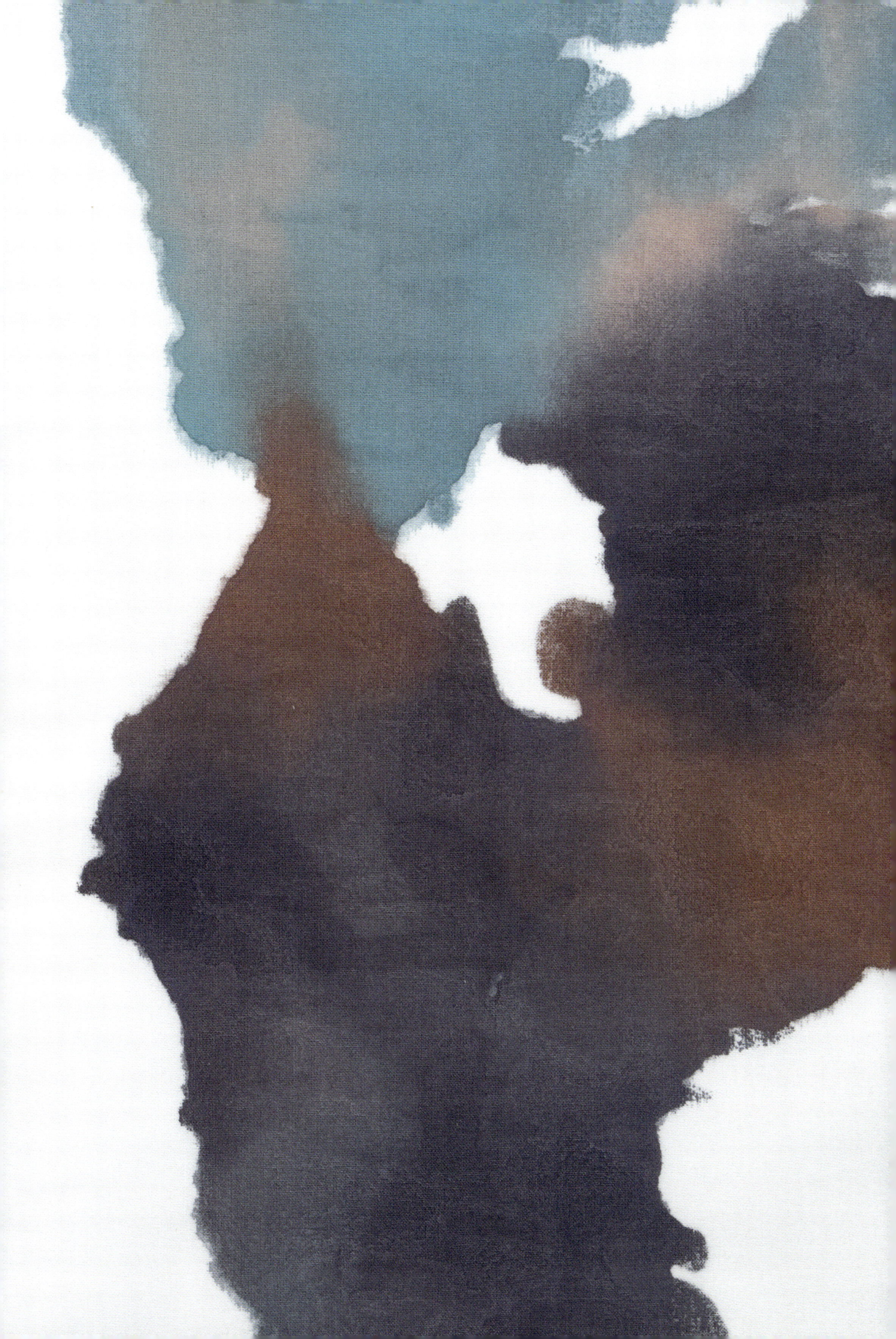

ritmo

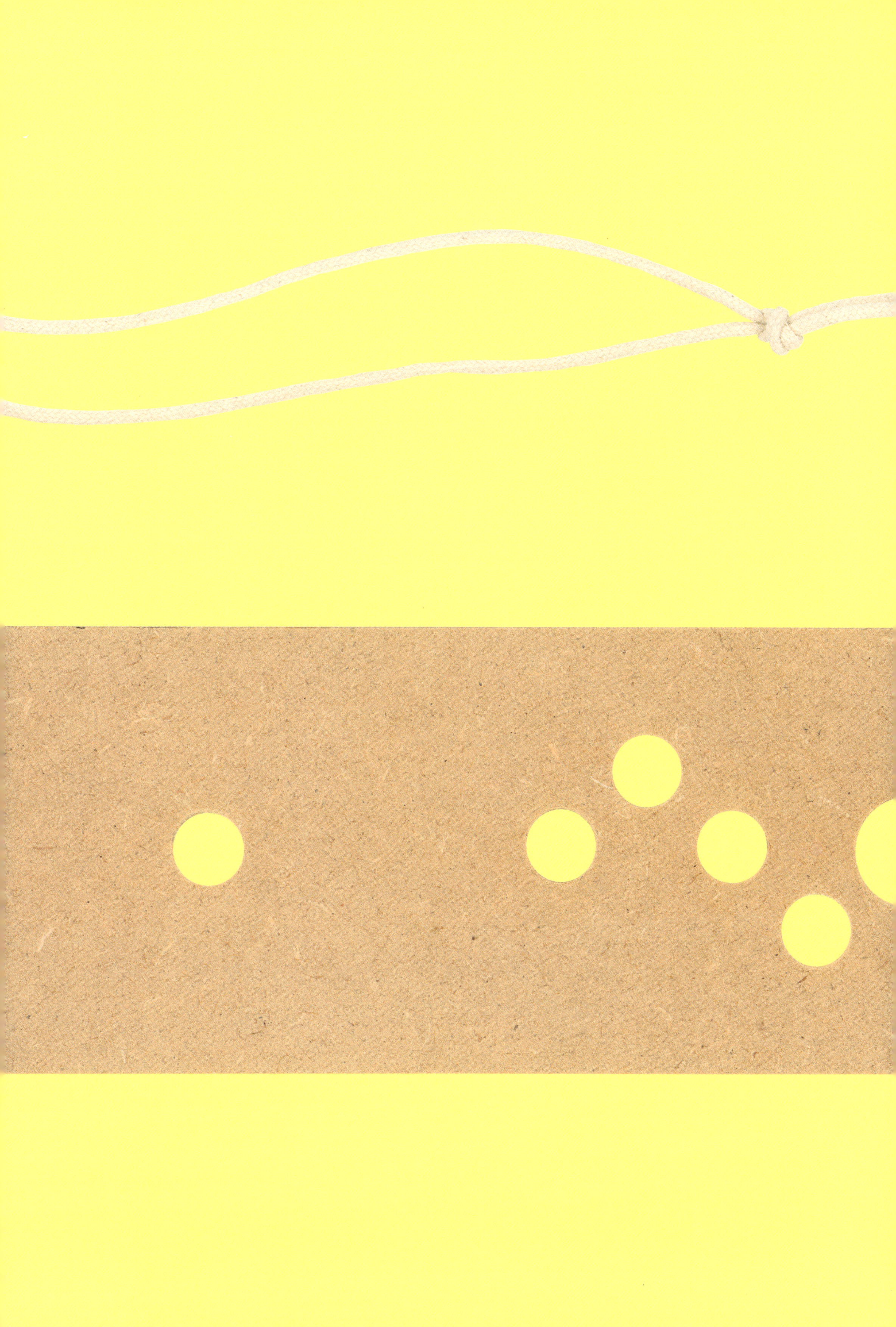

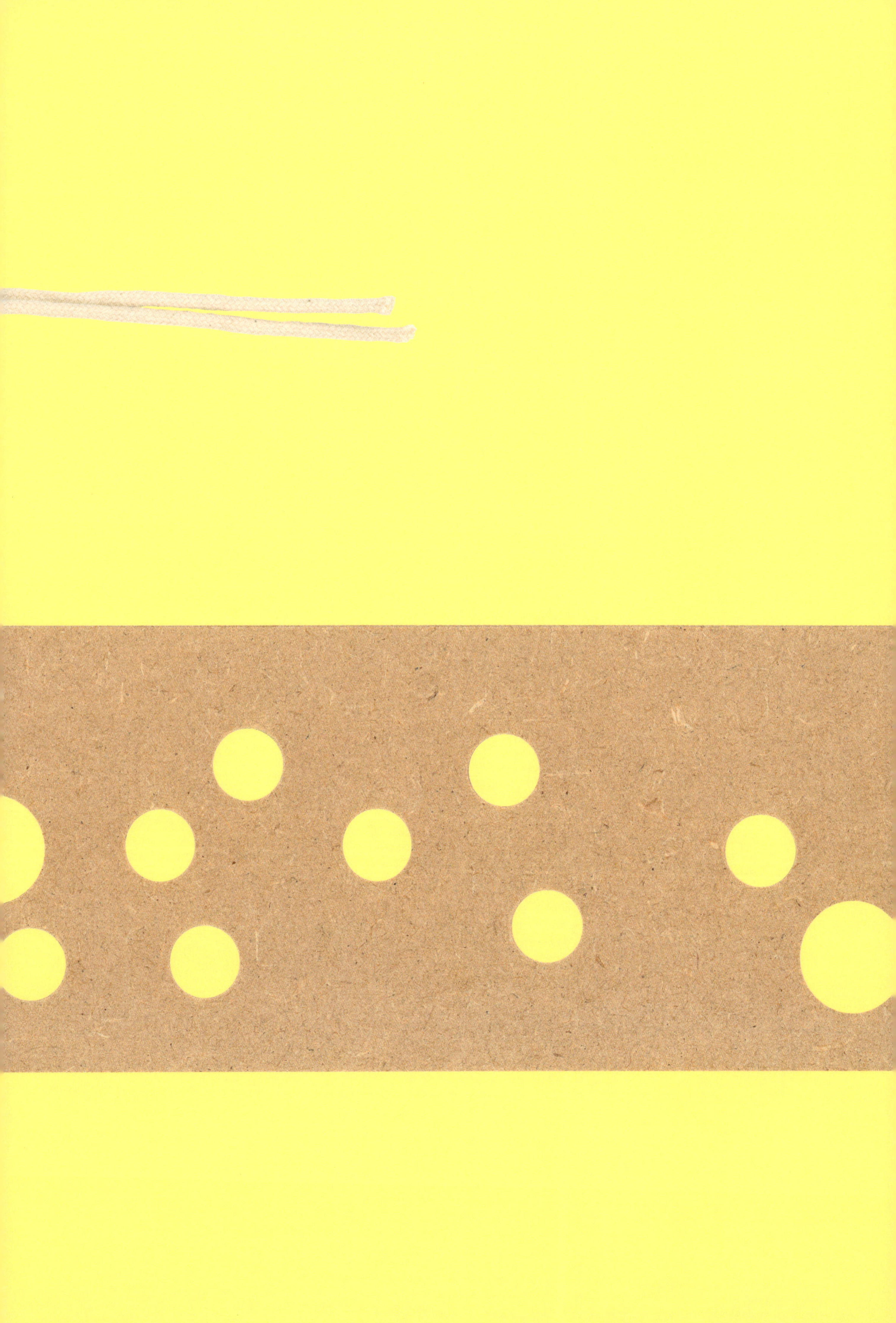

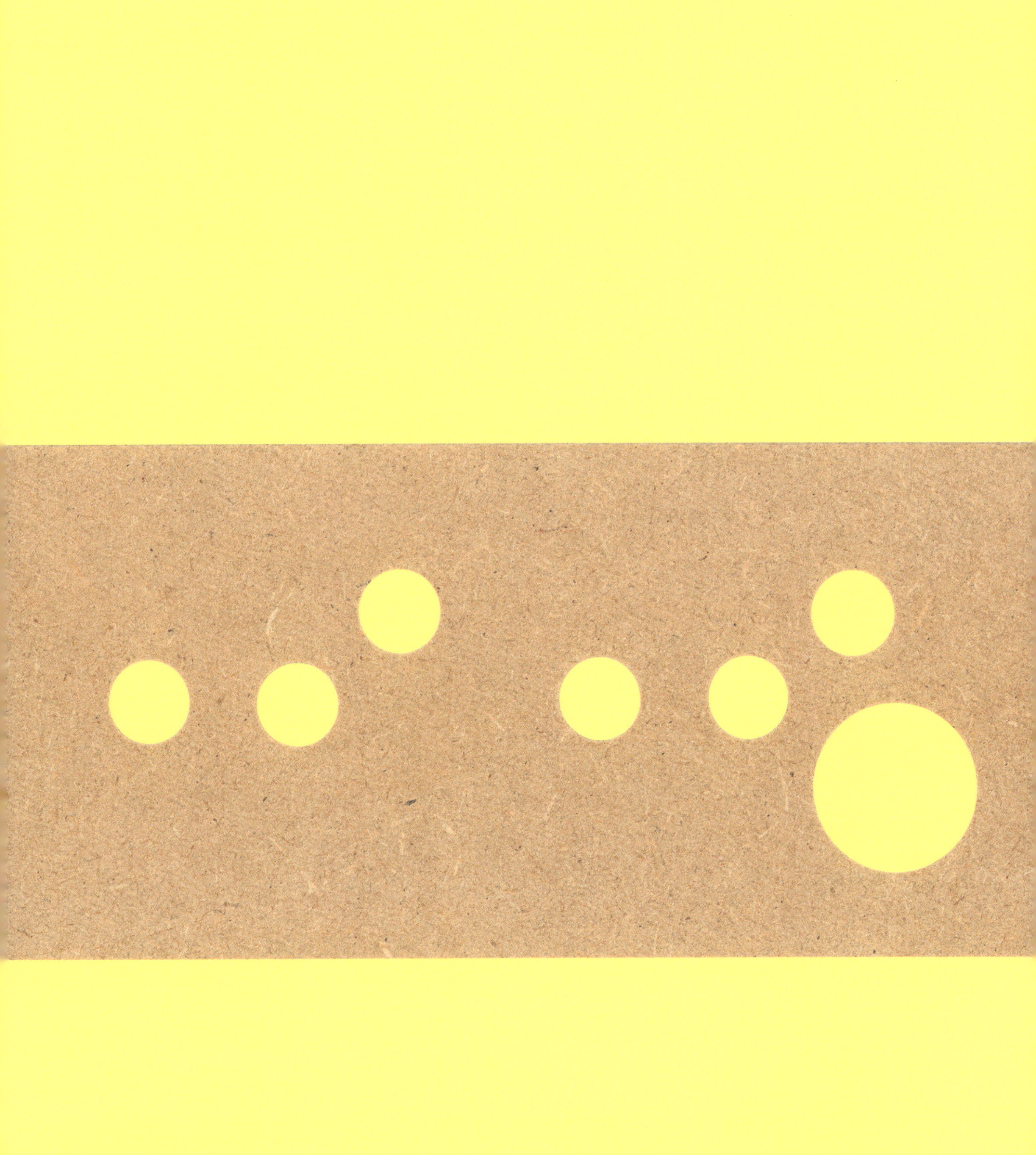

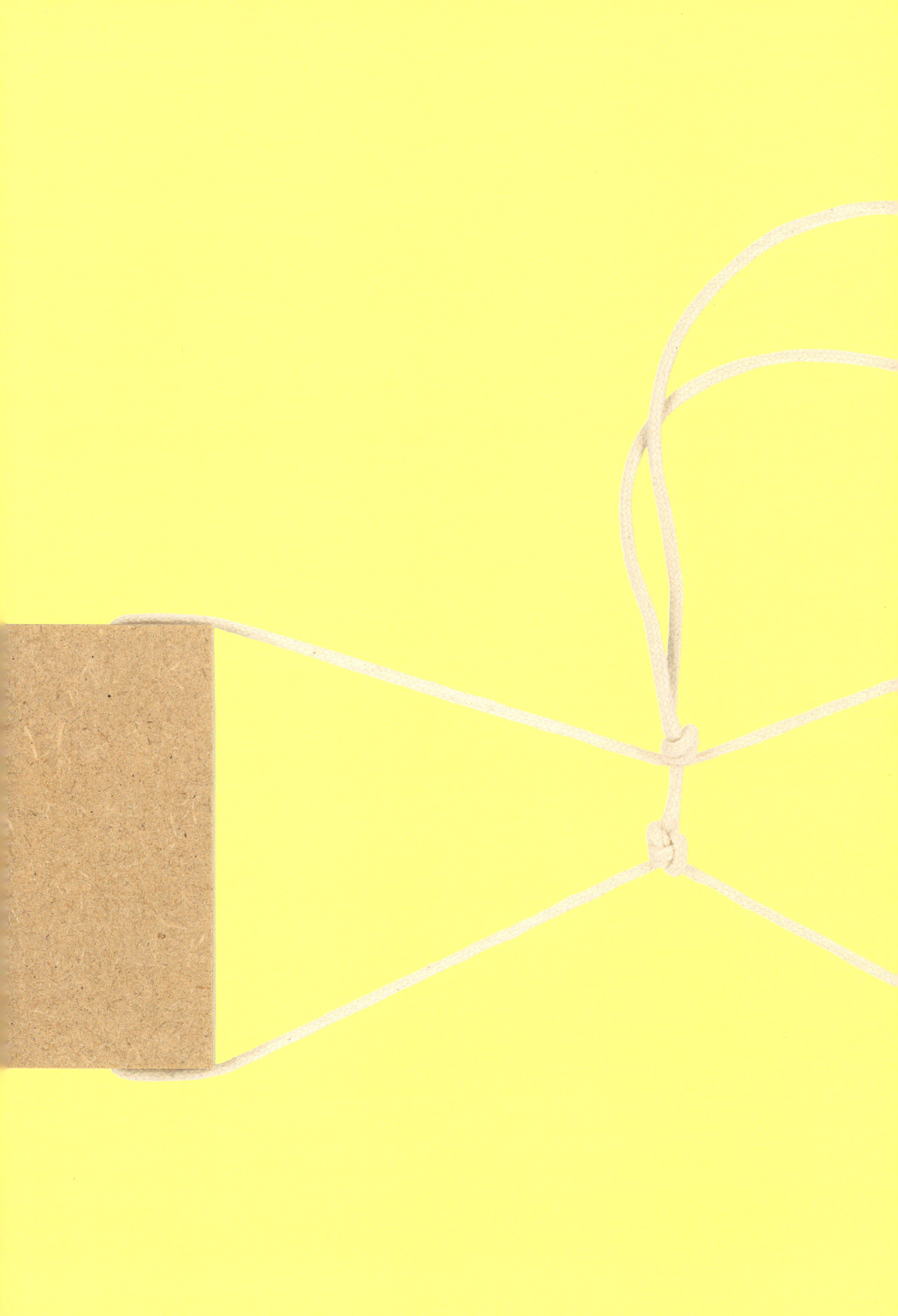

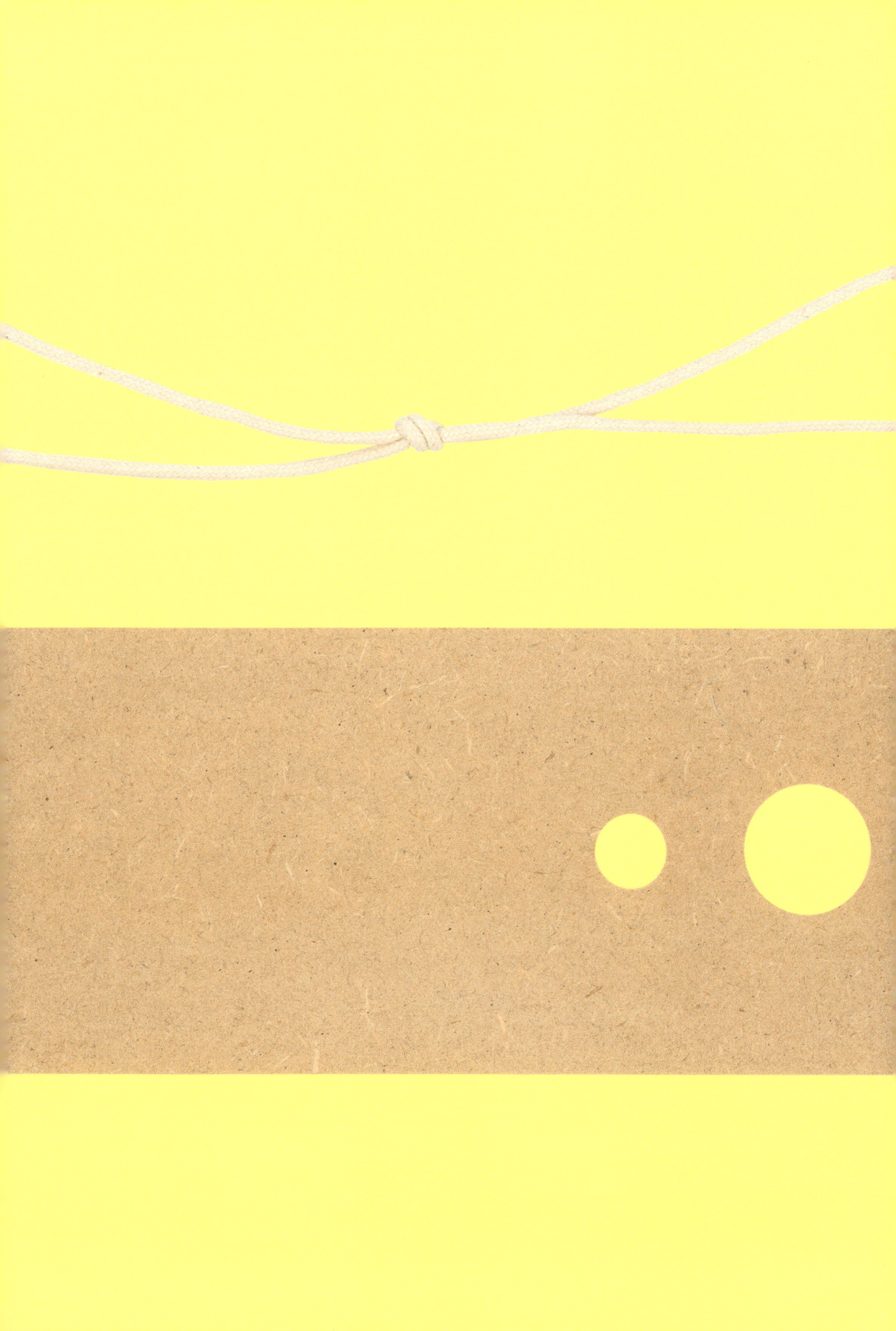

doppio movimento

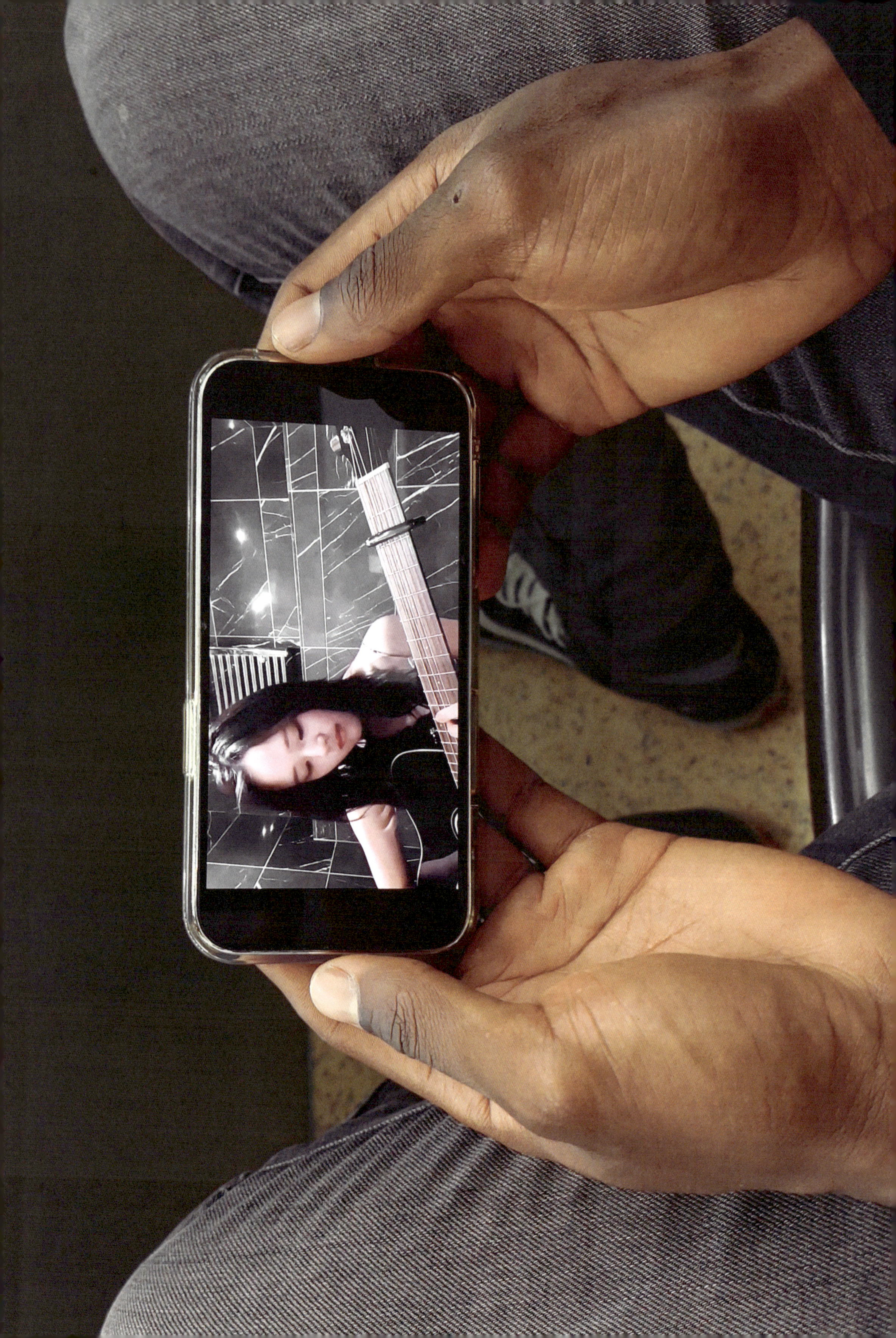

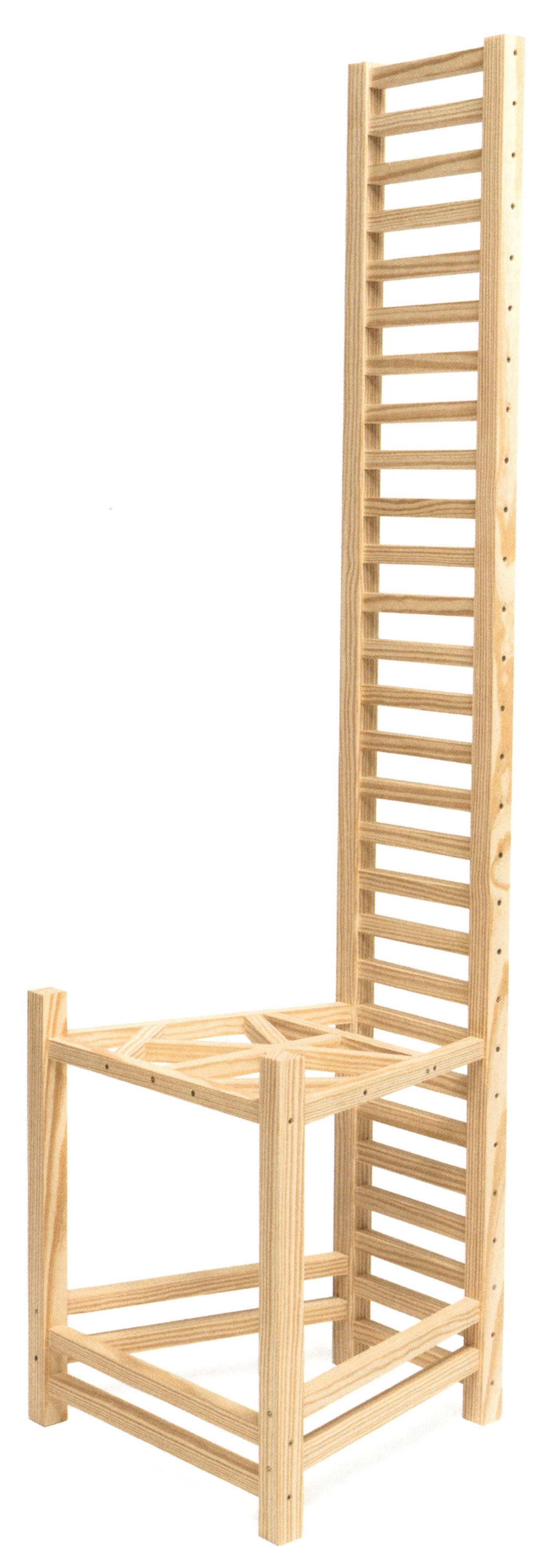

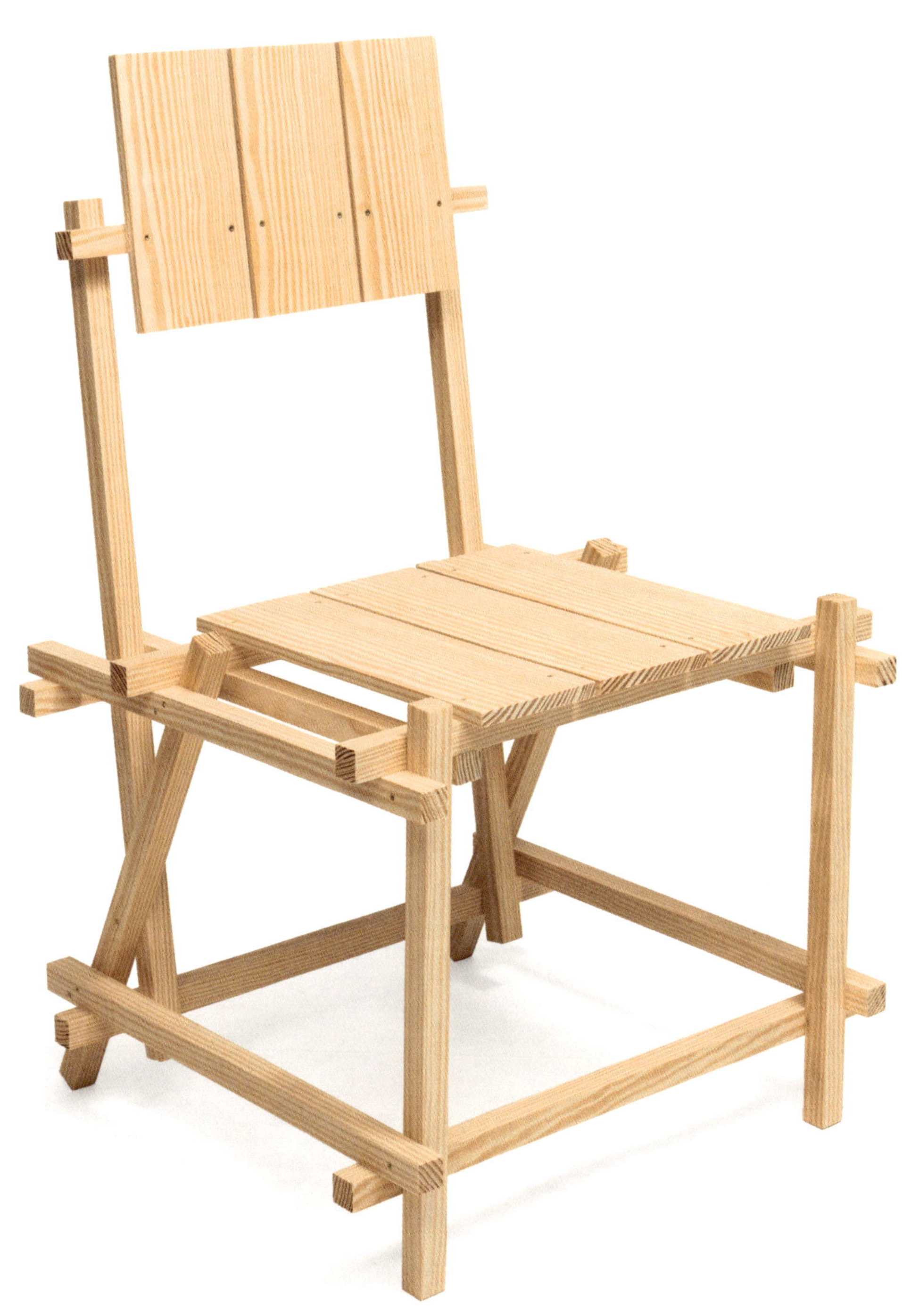

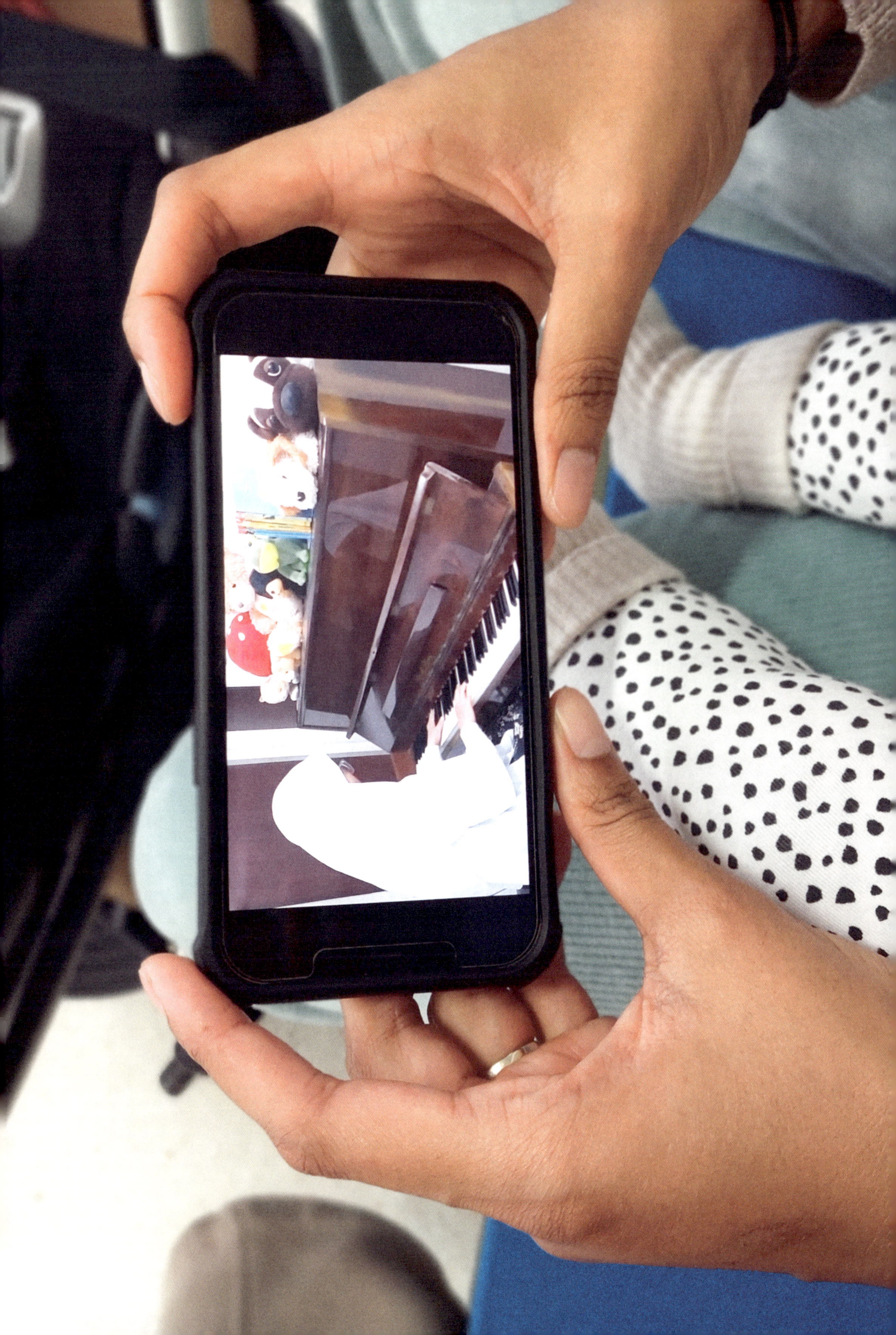

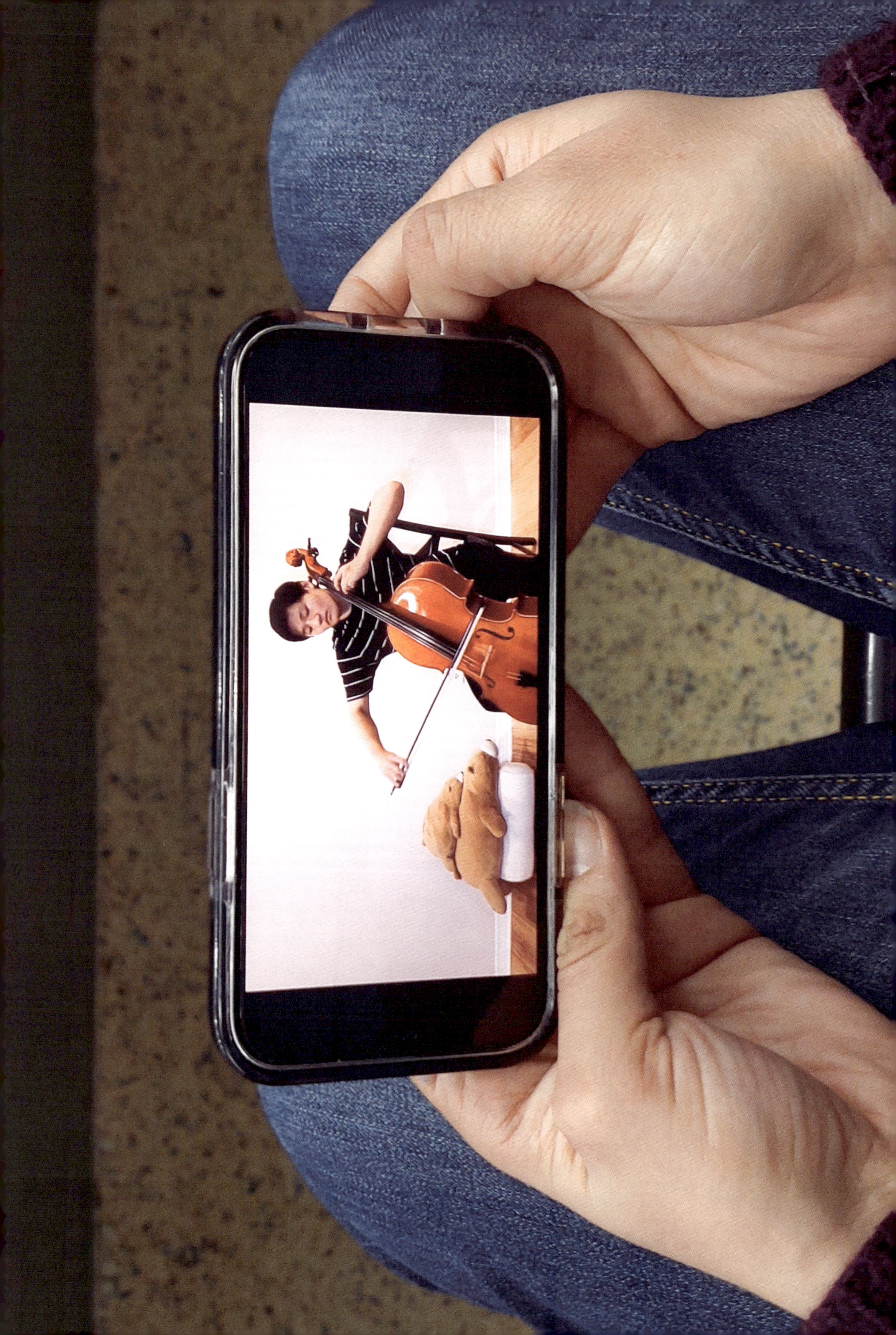

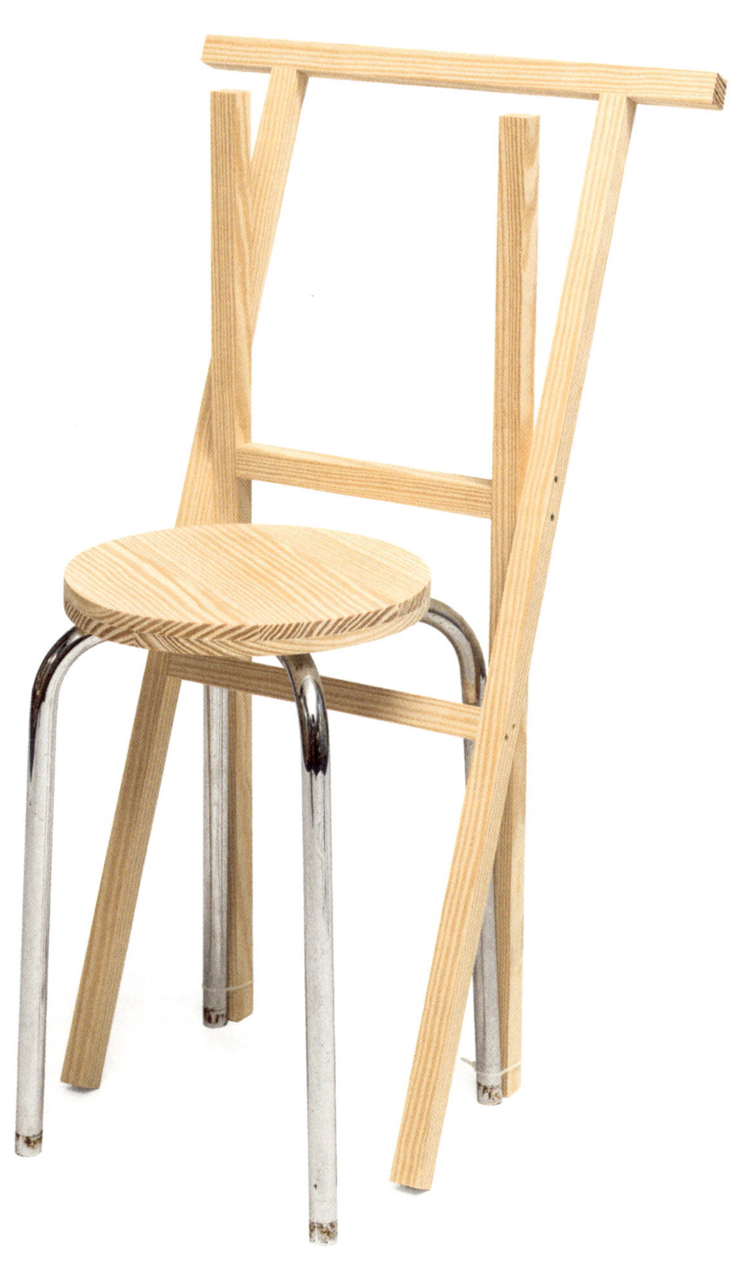

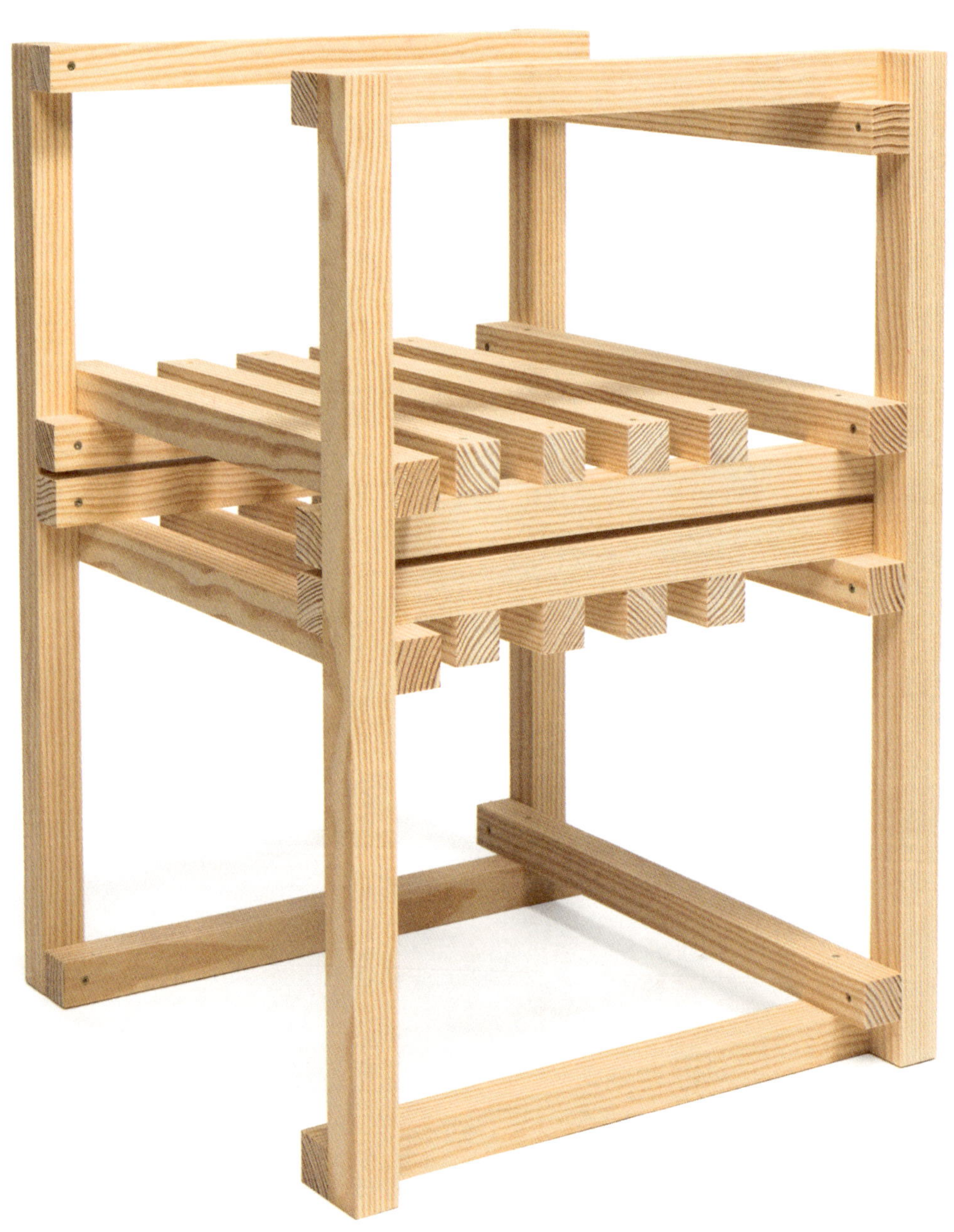

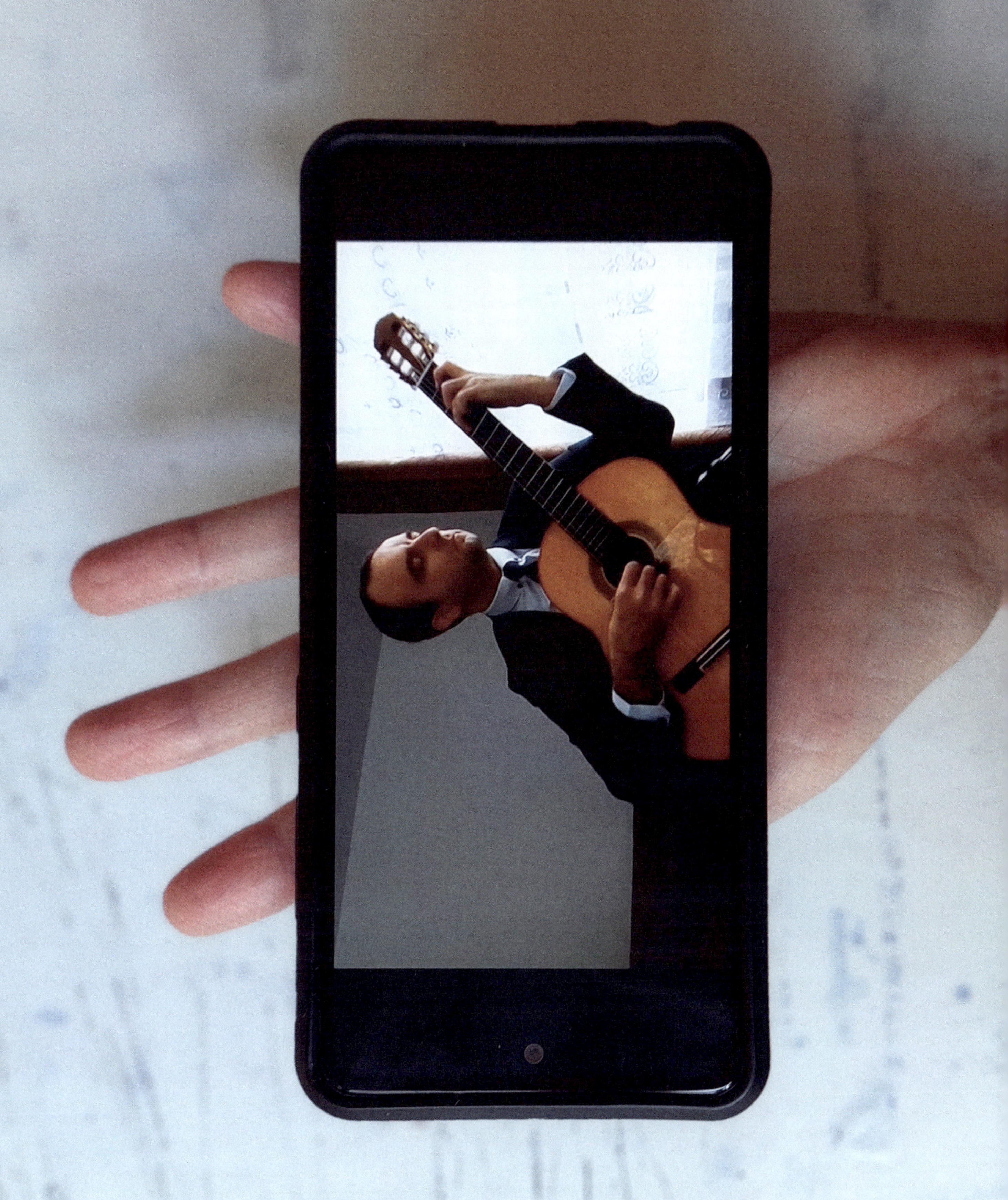

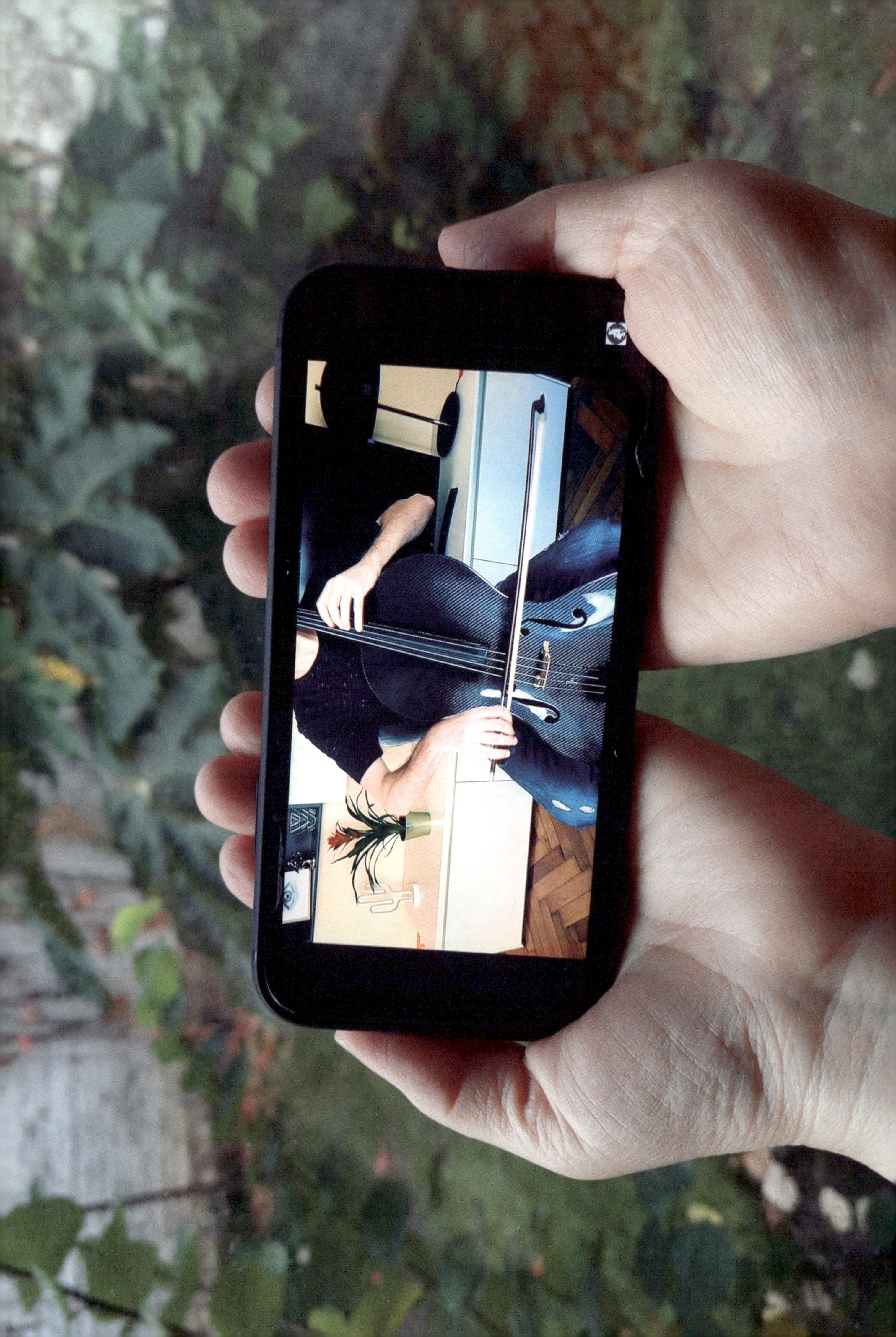

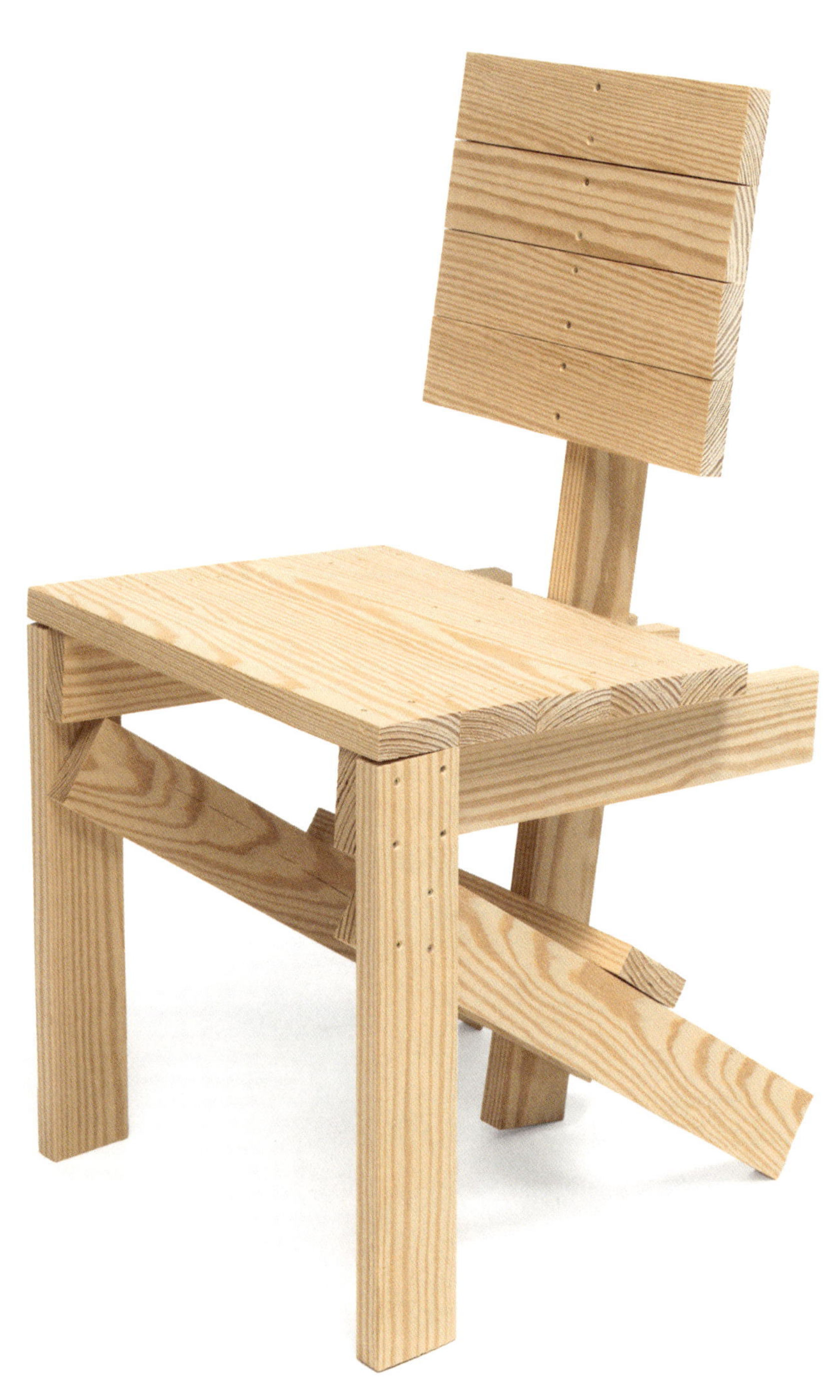

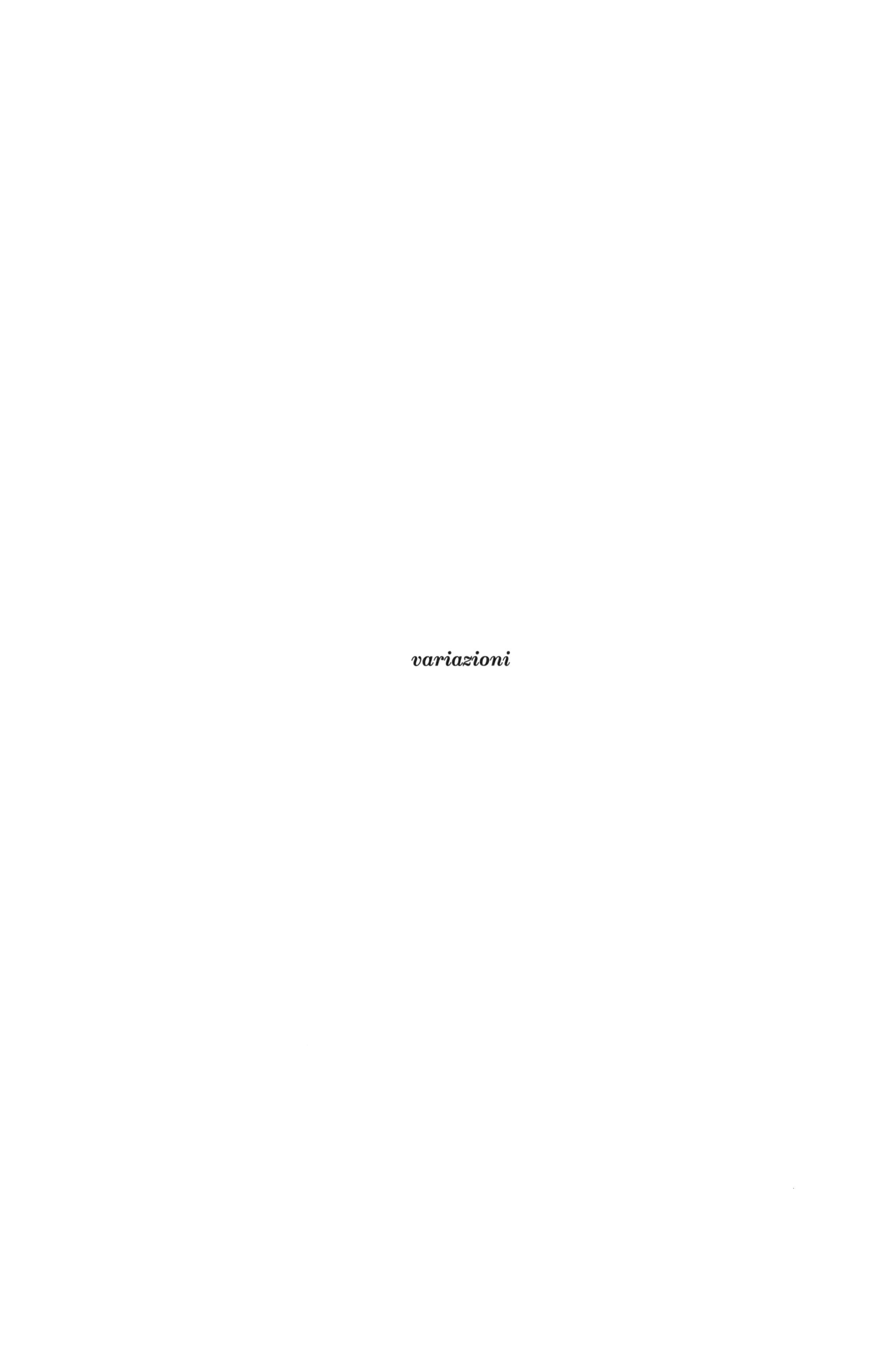

variazioni

TAMAR

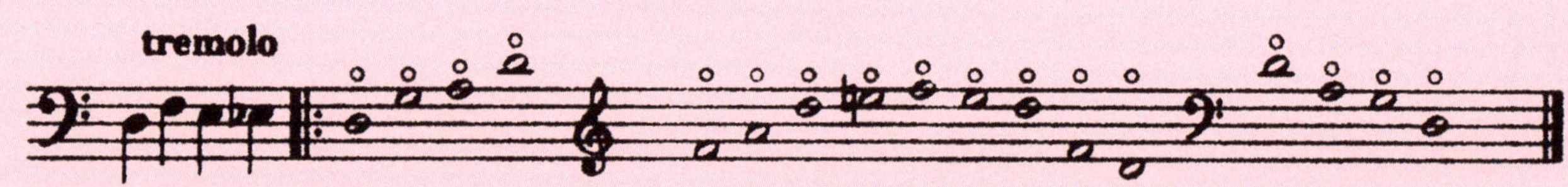

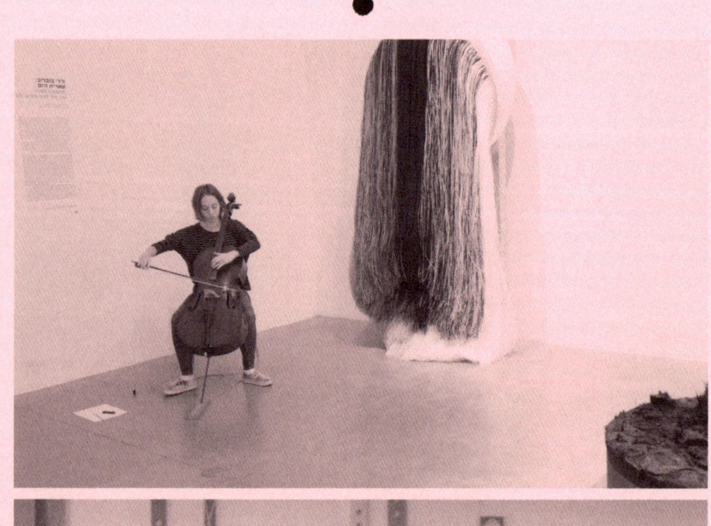

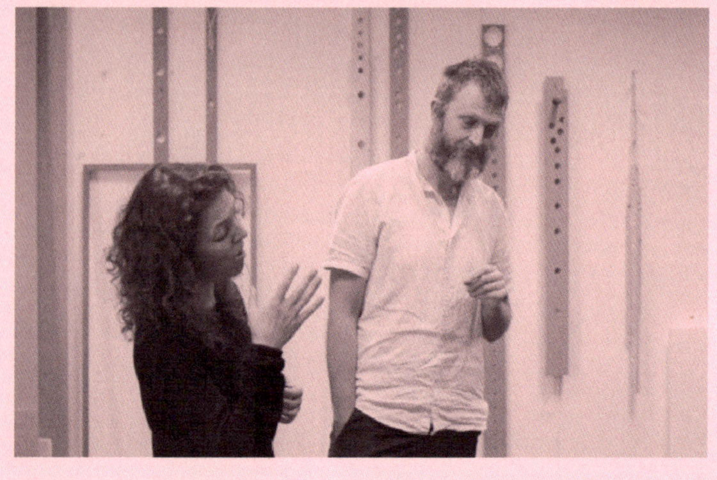

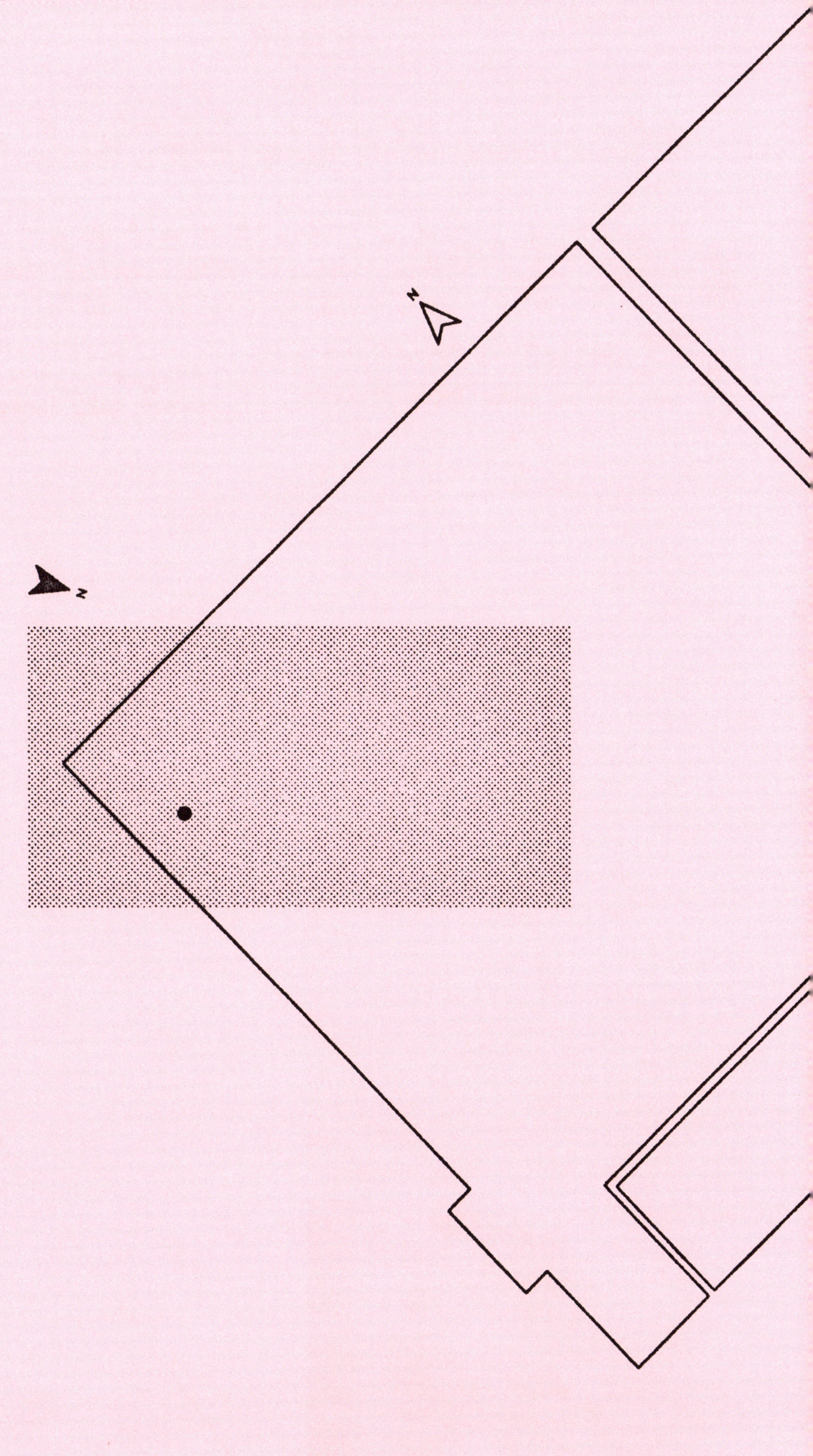
Studio
Museum

ERIK

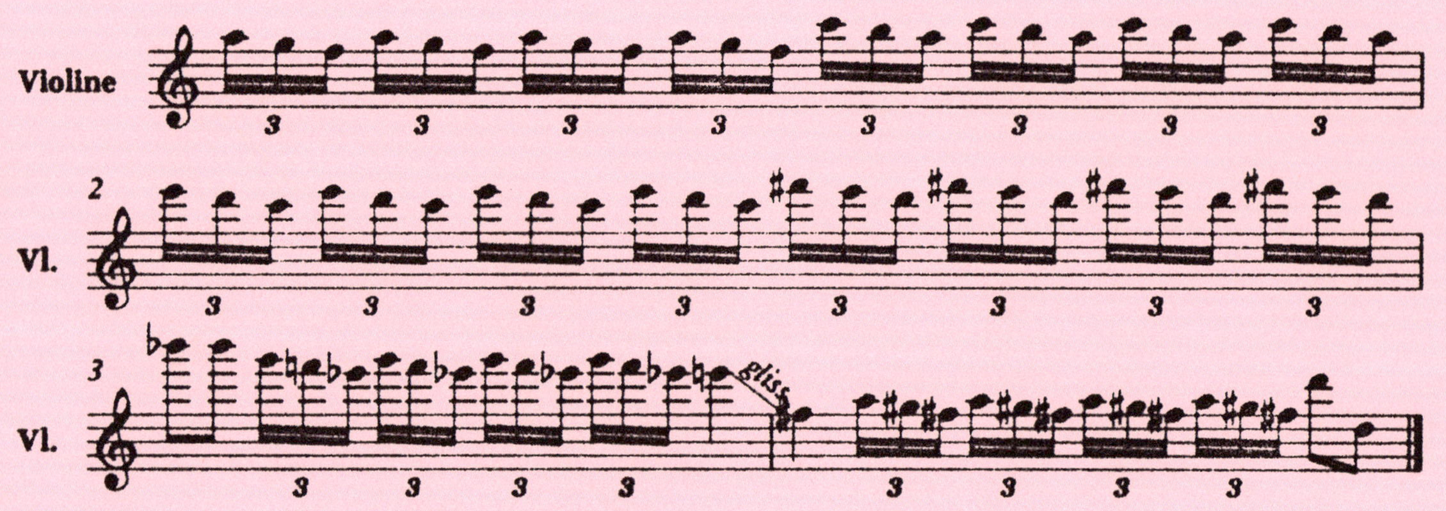

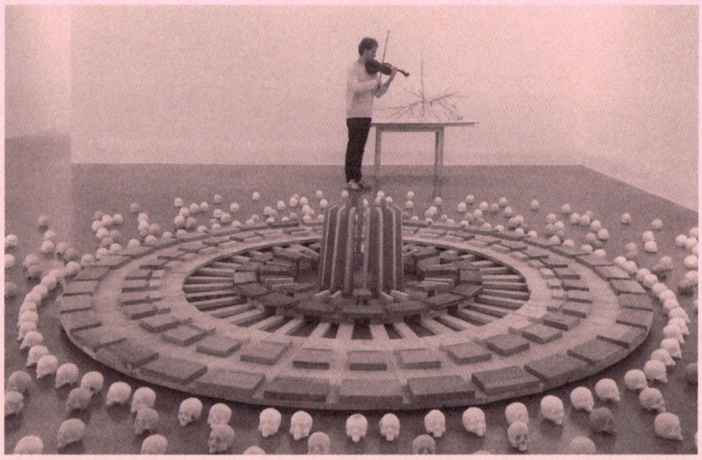

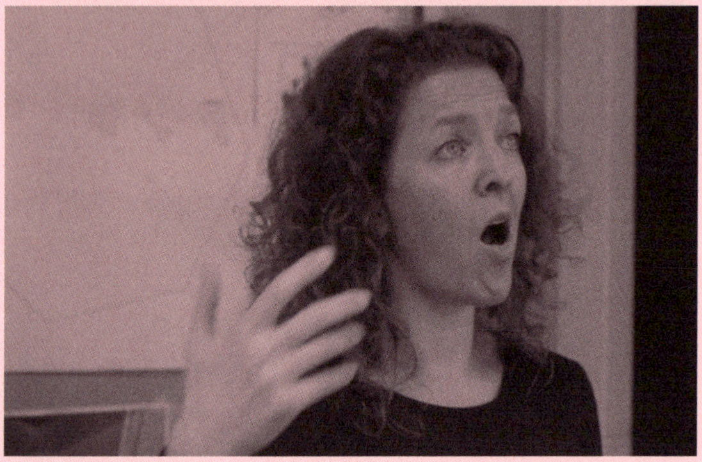

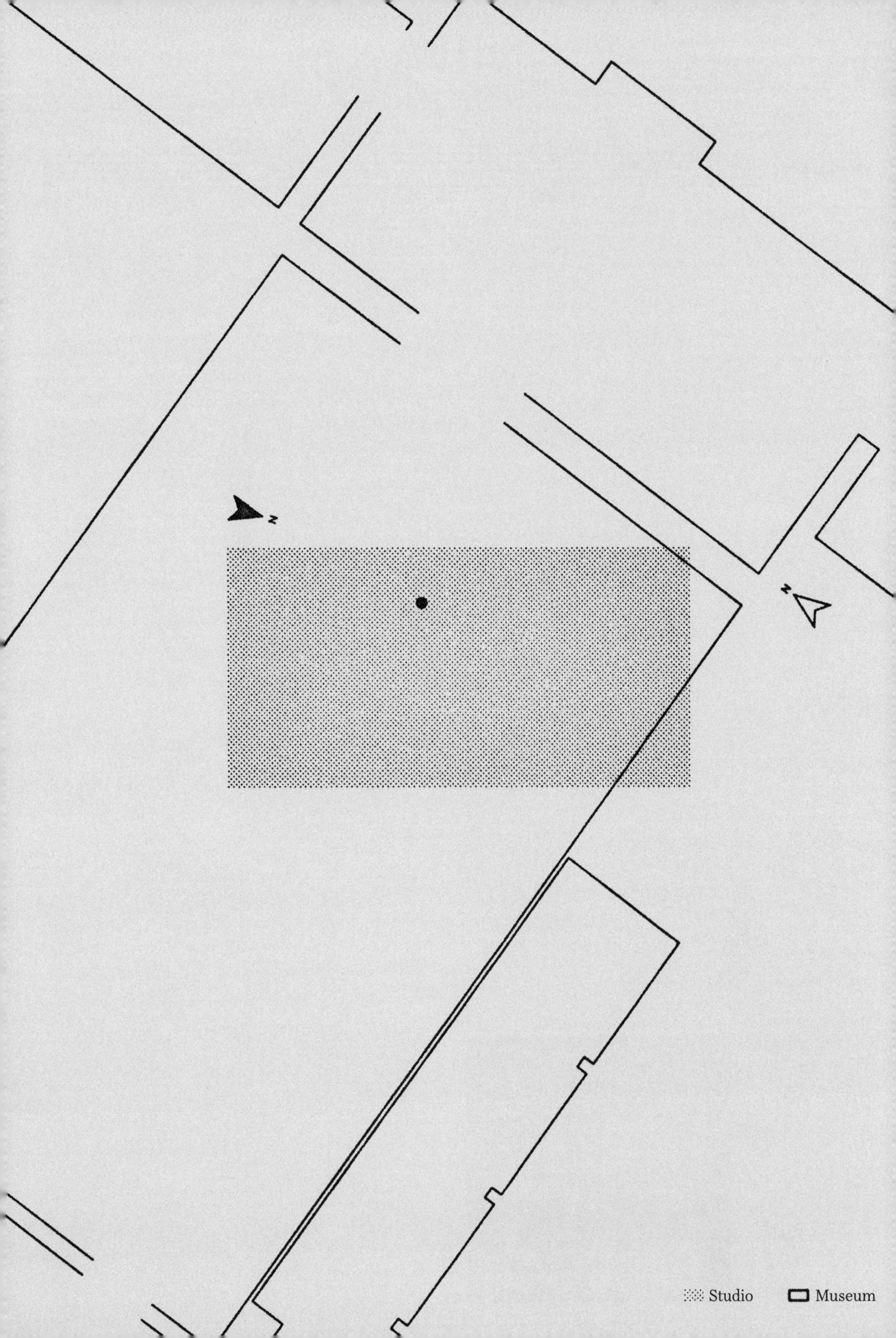

N
N
Studio
Museum

SHIRA

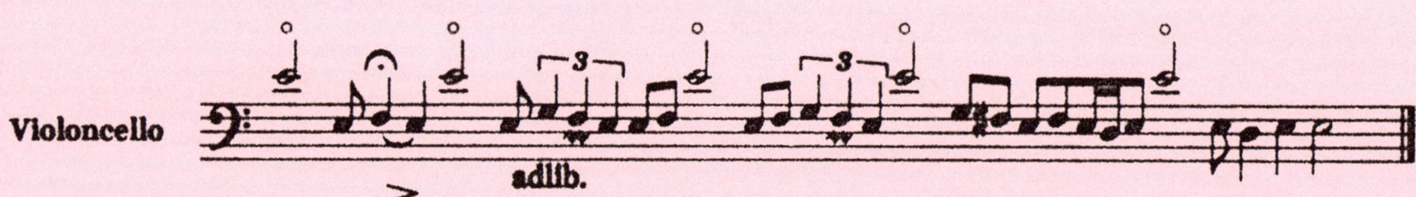

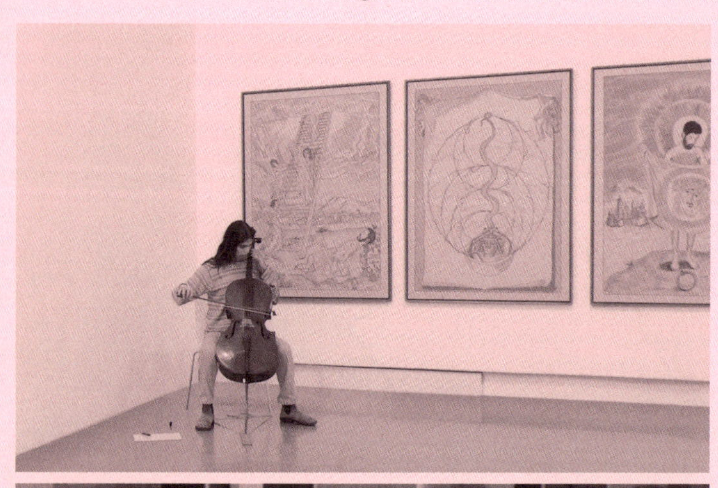

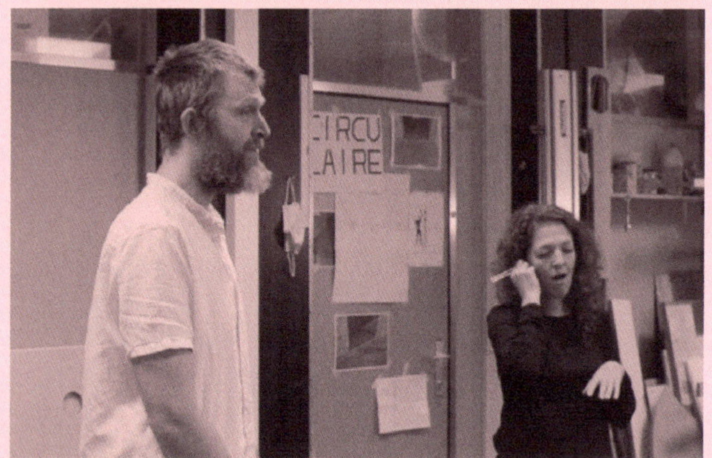

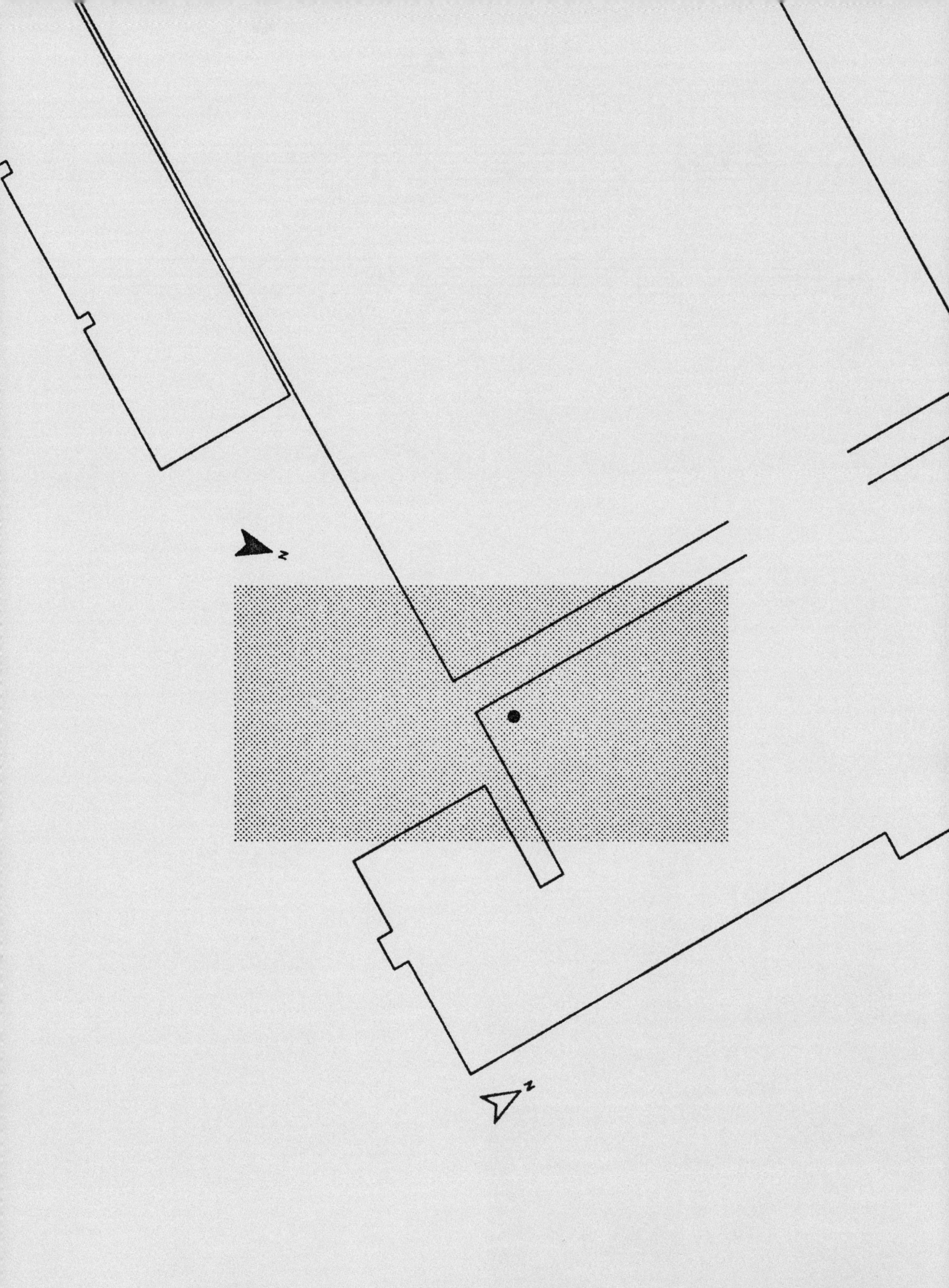

N
N
Studio
Museum

MICHAL

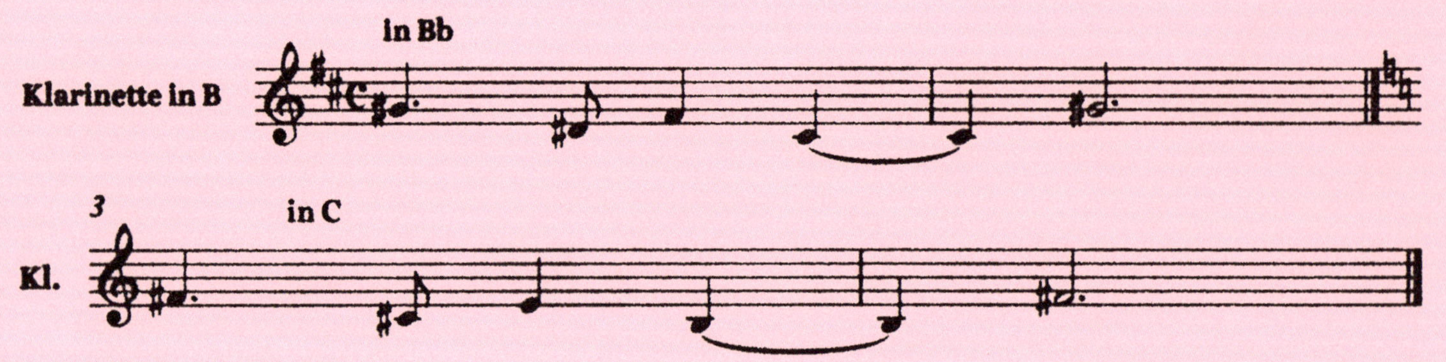

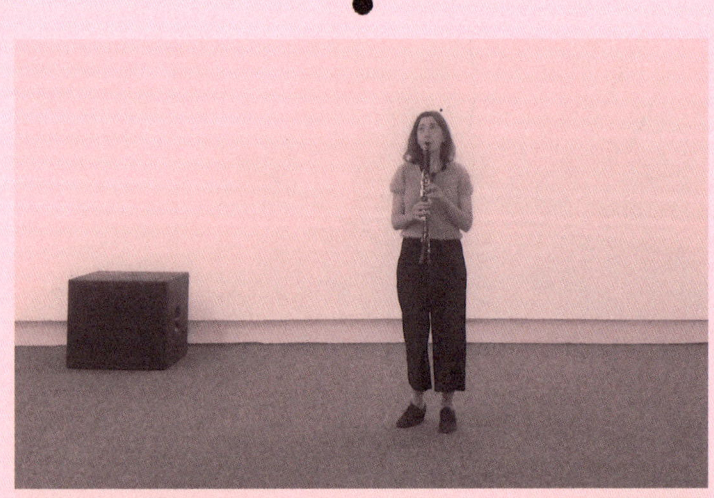

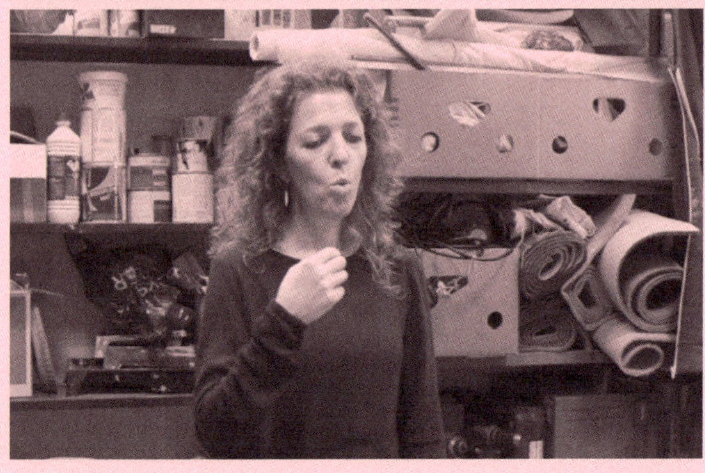

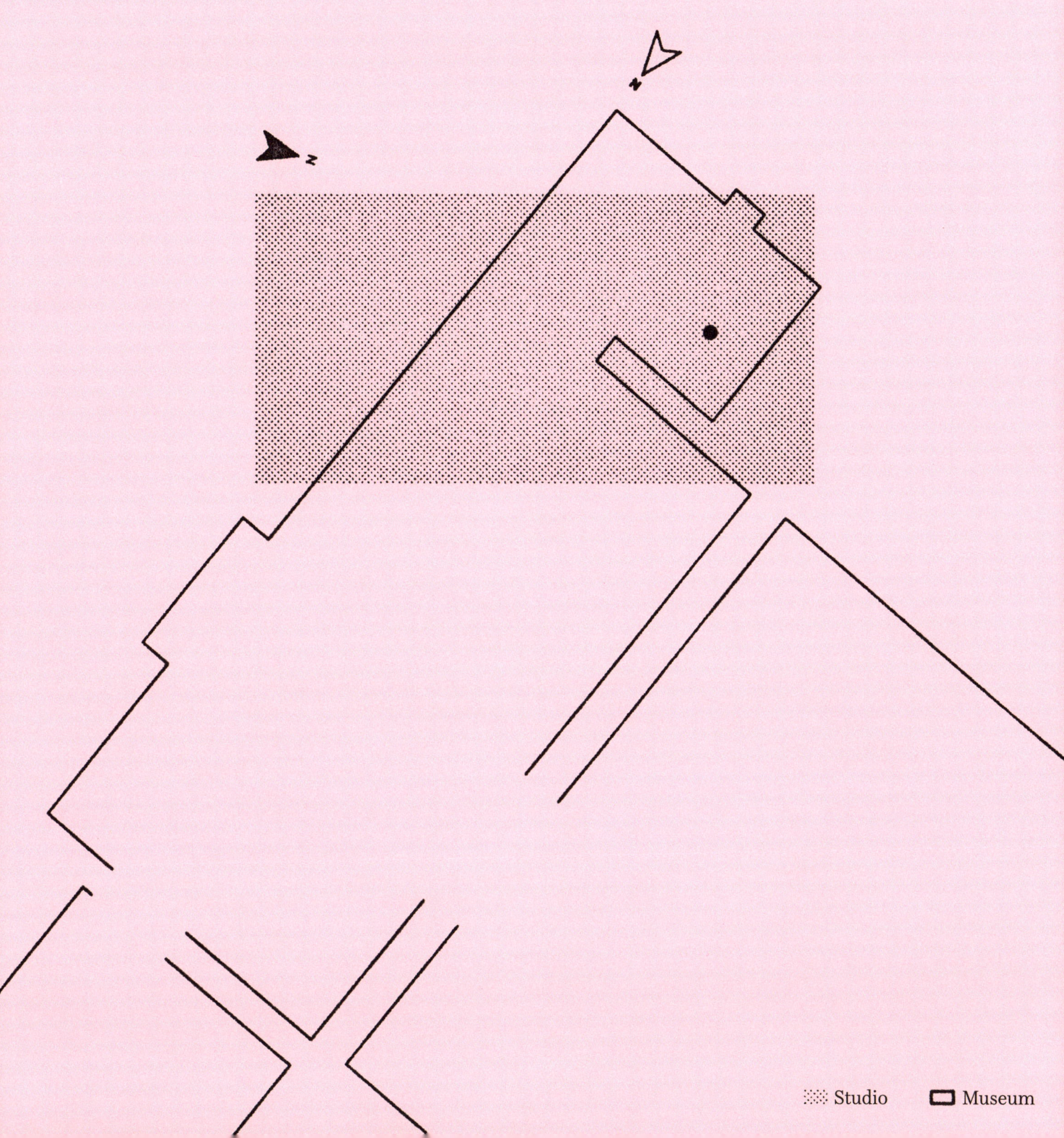
N
N
Studio
Museum

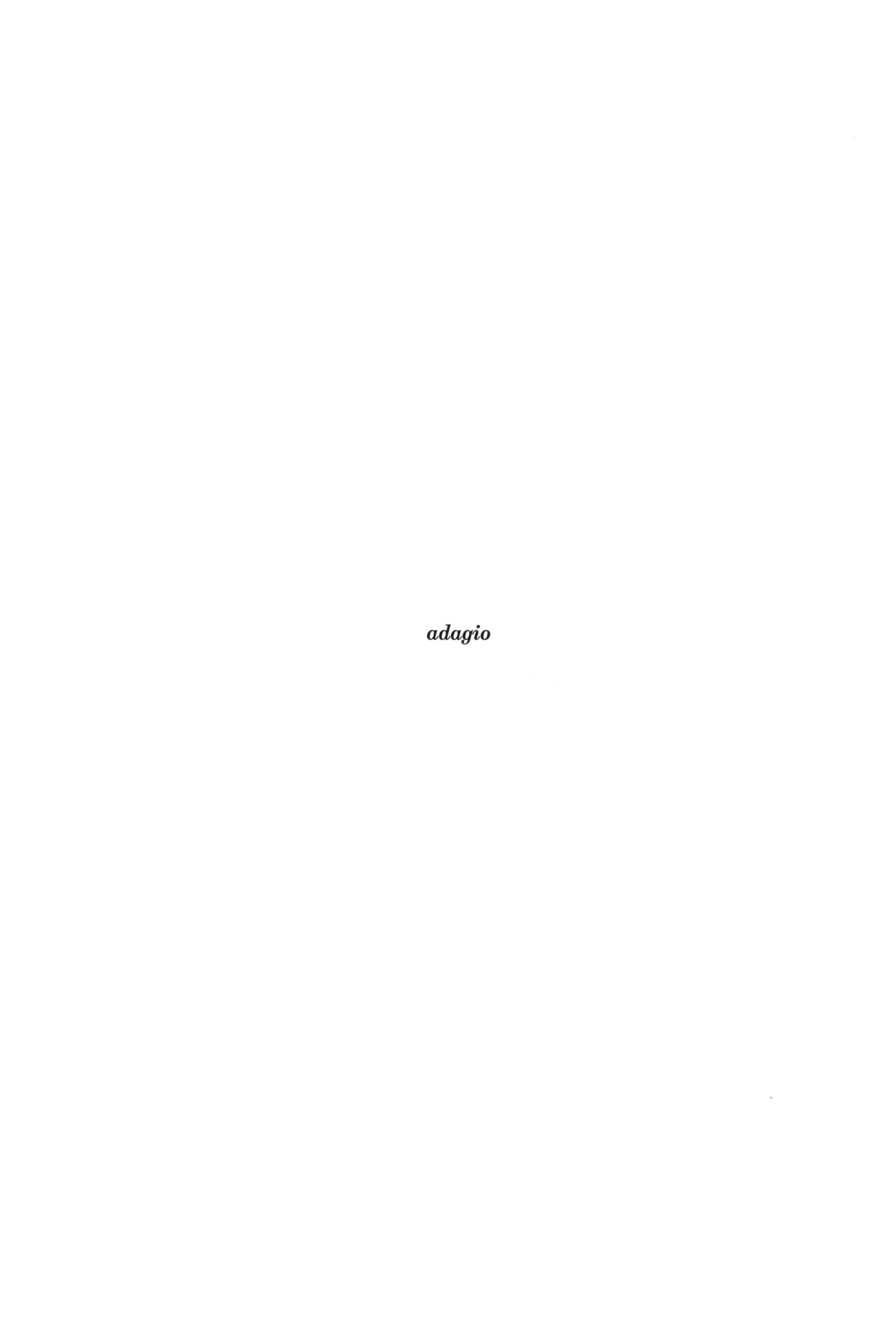

adagio

Listening to music is an experience that involves a person's entirety: body, mind, and emotions, placing the listener and the performer in a shared time and space; an act of being in the world. [02]

Petach Tikva Museum of Art created an opportunity to bring the worlds of classical music and visual art together to initiate a dialogue between them. In a unique tribute, the museum established an orchestra of its own, encouraging innovative interactions between visual artists and the orchestra. The exhibition "Incomplete Neighbor" proposes a different exchange between art and music, striving to transform the interactions between the parties involved in the process: the artists, the museum, and the orchestra.

In classical music, the term "incomplete neighbor tone" denotes a tone that is not always explicitly written, but its presence exists in our imagination, and is understood and felt through the context of the entire musical phrase. This gap between the absent and the present, the visual and the auditory, activates our imagination and senses and it is at the core of the exhibition. Bridging the gap calls for multiple interpretations, points of convergence, and anchors.

Like neighbors behind walls, who are not seen but whose actions are well heard, artists Raffaella Crispino (b. 1979, Italy; lives in Brussels, Belgium) and Hans Demeulenaere (b. 1974, Belgium; lives in Bruges, Belgium) initiated a dialogue with the orchestra members and communicated with them indirectly in a format called "Discourse," with the aim of prompting original modes of orchestral renditions. The artists sent sound files and open requests to the musicians, like an invitation to a dialogue. Their interaction with the musicians and with the museum space took on different forms, which led to the creation of the featured works.

Demeulenaere's point of departure for deciphering the relationship between the visual medium and the musical medium, is a study of the playing environment and the patterns that accompany the musicians such as the chairs they find comfortable, the endpin stoppers used to keep the musical instrument (cello) in place, and the points in the museum space where the music is heard best. The artist deconstructs and reconstructs all the elements into a visual expression that leaves signs and traces of the dialogue with the musicians in the space. Thus, for example, in the work *Prototypes*, Demeulenaere explored (formally and functionally) the chairs preferred by the musicians and created chairs in collaboration with art students inspired by iconic designers, such as Le Corbusier, Enzo Mari, Gerrit Rietveld, and Donald Judd. These references to the worlds of architecture, design, and visual art add another layer to the dialogue with the musical medium, mediating it into matter with the help of prevalent geometric principles (such as the Golden Ratio).

Demeulenaere refers to himself not as an "artist," but as a "translator," who reconstructs, reflects, and studies things in the world. The engagement with translation between the verbal, musical, and visual art languages in many of the featured works conjures up Walter Benjamin's comments about the "task of the translator": "a translation, instead of resembling the meaning of the original, must lovingly and in detail incorporate the original's mode of signification, thus making both the original and the translation recognizable as fragments of a greater language, just as fragments are part of a vessel."[03]

The exhibition sheds light on the set of associations forming in relation to the point of departure. It raises questions about what is lost in transition between the starting point and the resulting free interpretation, encouraging creativity on the part of all participants in the process.

All the works on view contain a gap or leap. Thus, for instance, in *A Room With a Voice*, the orchestra is instructed to "improvise a perfect musical phrase," and to "listen to the soundscape." Each musician looks for the points in the museum which, they believe, allow for the optimal sound. According to Michal Oren, musical director and conductor of the Museum Orchestra, while composing the "perfect phrase," the musicians were inspired by the works of art and the contents presented in the space at the time. The resulting musical phrases were recorded and sent back to the artist in Bruges, where professional singers listened to those phases and recorded an audio version of the music pieces in Demeulenaere's studio. The recording also captured the ambient noises and the studio's sound-space. The work thus develops in a spiral movement, each move in the dialogue adding sound content to the basic theme, which can develop and create a small but significant change, increasingly inspiring the work with the artist's character. In the very instruction, in the transition between artists and musicians, there is a point of "loss of control." What is lost in translation forms raw material for a new work that manifests itself in the environmental effects.

The exhibition "Incomplete Neighbor" explores how our mind complements the reality around us, how visual art and music activate our mind and trigger it to create ideas, thoughts, and feelings.

When Crispino moved to Brussels in 2011, she experienced difficulties creating visual works, and instead taught herself to play the Omnichord—an electronic musical instrument introduced in the 1980s. Over the course of some 18 months, she adopted a daily practice of composing songs, which were named after the date of their creation. The result was a vinyl album, *Ogni Giorno* (It. every day), which is a musical diary. The recorded songs were "translated" by the artists to the color system developed by Japanese artist and designer Sanzo Wada in his *Dictionary of Color Combinations*, associating colors with the seasons. Titled *Libretto*,[04] the work is presented in the exhibition in such a way that viewers listen to the record while looking at the multiplicity of colored fabrics in the space and are invited to "join" the idiosyncrasies of color, sound, and time to generate a new translation in their imagination.

Another gap that our imagination bridges arises when Crispino tries to decipher the power of music as a catalyst for the expression of emotion and communication between people. Following personal conversations with orchestra members, she initiated *Teaching Emotions*. Each musician was given a musical piece by a composer of their choice to perform while receiving instructions from Oren, the orchestra's musical director and conductor, who asked them to heighten and express the feelings embedded in the piece. The performing musician and the conductor were recorded separately, and museum visitors can listen to the music played in one space and to musical instructions in another space, thus realizing the idea of the "incomplete neighbor" as the visitors listen, respond, and contemplate each element separately as well as their coupling. Moreover, the musical instructions are given in Italian (e.g., legato, staccato, forte, etc.), which is the universal language of music, but the foreign accent in which they are pronounced infuses the musical renditions with a local tone.

Music as a generator of emotion is emphasized in the work *All the Ways We Love*. In the background, the question arises: must one experience love to properly play a love song? (as teachers often guide their students before a musical performance). In this work, Crispino invites viewers to take part in playing a musical collage of love expressions, consisting of amateur and professional performances of the same melody.[05] The emotion "trickles" from the performers' personal room into the public space, emphasizing the power of music as a universal language that bridges cultures and reveals emotions common in human nature.

In many cases, a contradiction arises between the visual and the auditory, between the exhibition visitors, who observe and listen to the melodramatic singers, and the musicians, whose playing ostensibly begs the viewers to feel an emotion that is foreign to the museum context in which it is played. Visitors are invited to play additional musical renditions of the same love song and create a dialogue with the other voices played in the exhibition space. The polyphony gives rise to additional interpretations of the original melody.

The theme "incomplete neighbor" is a catalyst for actions that are like musical ripples, moving away from the starting point and concluding as another whole. The collaboration between Crispino and Demeulenaere brings different ways of expressing this idea to the fore. Crispino begins by "getting lost in the incomprehensible," the chaotic, paving her path by intuition, feelings, and instincts—a Dionysian process. Whereas Demeulenaere begins his artistic process in an Apollonian structured and calculated manner, sometimes relying on iconic references, which are gradually unraveled during the interpretive-discursive movement and the development of the works. Together, they offer a holistic view of the relations between auditory art and visual art which is created via dialogue with music and inspired by it.

The works in the exhibition are the result of a chain of actions that oscillate between the covert and overt, referring to something without spelling it out explicitly. The open nature of the subject and the numerous possibilities generated by the dialectic between the distinct and the implicit are a significant part of the exhibition, which invites visitors to listen to the music of the other's language.

01.   The essay was inspired by a conversation between Nirith Nelson, the project's initiator and creator of the exhibition concept, artists Raffaella Crispino and Hans Demeulenaere, and Tal Bechler, the exhibition curator, held on October 28, 2022.
02.   See Jean-Luc Nancy, *Listening*, trans. Charlotte Manadell (New York: Fordham UP, 2007).
03.   Walter Benjamin, "The Task of the Translator," in *Illuminations*, ed. Hannah Arendt, trans. Harry Zohn (New York: Harcourt Brace Jovanovich, 1968), p. 78.
04.   A libretto (It. booklet) contains the text for musical theater as well as drawings.
05.   "Tema d'Amore" (Love Theme, 1989) from the soundtrack of *Cinema Paradiso*; music by Ennio Morricone.

pianissimo

TEACHING EMOTIONS

In a video call between the conductor
and the musician, the conductor asked
the musician to name a composer
that they like, after which the conductor chose a piece by this composer.
The musician then played the piece
while being conducted by musical
terms (i.e. lento, crescendo, etc.)
that the conductor instructed. In
the installation, one speaker plays the
piece that the musician performed.
In a separate room, a second speaker
plays the voice of the conductor
instructing musical terms. Visitors
are invited to combine the two halves
in their imagination while they walk
through the space.

I WOULD LOVE
TO BE A PAINTER

This video is a recording of a conversation in sign language between a man
and a woman, seated by the window
of an apartment across the street.
The relationship between the two of
them is unclear but you can see from
their proximity and body language
that they're having an intimate
conversation. The text that appears
in the video could be a transcription
of their conversation, but it could
also be the musings of the artists
making the recording. The text
describes the longing to be a painter,
to have a brushstroke that makes an
artist recognizable through a gesture.
It describes the struggles of being
a conceptual artist and the loneliness
of trying to communicate without
ever being certain that you're being
understood. The work is an explora-
tion of language and the loss of poetry
created in the way we converse with
one another – as artists, musicians,
and people.

ALL THE WAYS
WE LOVE

Since 2010 Raffaella has been collec-
ting YouTube videos of people playing
«Il tema d'amore» (Love Theme)
from Ennio Morricone's soundtrack
for the film «Nuovo Cinema Paradiso»
on different instruments. There are
also people singing its later version
"Se", which has lyrics. The covers are
done by amateurs and professionals,
and Raffaella saw in them an attempt
to show feelings of love through their
performance. In this way, they are
digital serenades that blend private
and public space, recorded in domes-
tic settings but uploaded for anyone

to access. Visitors can play these
videos in the exhibition space on their
mobile phones in an orchestral spatial
organisation and watch each video
alone or in cacophony with other
visitors' phones.

PROTOTYPES

In this work, Hans asked five
musicians to think about the chair
on which they spend the most time
playing. They were asked to document
it in three photos (front, side and
from above) and measure it.
He paired each of their chairs with
a chair made by an architect or
designer to create a new piece that
is a balance between a sculpture and
a prototype for a new chair. Hans's
pieces are unique; *Charles*, *Gerrit*,
Philippe, *Donald* and *Mario*. They are
not made to be reproduced or even
used as a chair. They are autonomous
objects that could lead to possible new
designs. This work can be compared
to the way a musician performs
a score – a unique interpretation is
necessary to make music come alive.

RULERS

An endpin stopper is a device that is
placed between a cello's endpin (the
rod at the bottom of the instrument)
and the floor to prevent the cello from
slipping while it's being played. They
are lengths of wood with multiple
holes, which allow the cellist to choose
a position that is most comfortable.
Some designs secure to the chair with
a cord or are foldable. When Hans
saw the stoppers used by cellists Shira
and Tamar, he was struck by the
stoppers' resemblance to rulers.
This work is a series of pieces inspired
by both stoppers and rulers.
The measurements of the holes are
based on personal systems developed
by architects and designers such
as Le Corbusier, Donald Judd, Enzo
Mari, and Gerrit Rietveld. One such
system is the Modulor, devised
by Le Corbusier, which is a scale
of proportions based on the height
of a man with his arm raised.
With variations in the size and position of the holes, and length and
thickness of the wood, the pieces can
be used as endpin stoppers and rulers,
but can also be read as scores if
the holes are interpreted as notes.

LIBRETTO

A libretto (Italian for "booklet")
contains the text for musical theatre

as well as drawings. In this work,
Hans and Raffaella created their own
libretto based on "Ogni Giorno", an
album of thirteen songs composed and
performed by Raffaella. Each piece
is named with the date on which it was
created. The songs were matched
with colors from a color system
connected to the seasons developed
by Japanese artist and designer Sanzo
Wada. They poured ink in the chosen
colors on light cotton fabric. New
colors and shapes formed when the
fabric was folded in half and pressed.
The result is a series of thirteen
mirrored images that echo the inkblot
tests of psychiatrist Hermann
Rorschach. They chose this technique
out of a desire to include chance
in their work.

OGNI
GIORNO

When Raffaella moved to Brussels
in 2011, she found herself unable to
produce visual work. As an alternative,
she began a daily practice of composing music that continued for more
than a year and a half. She taught
herself to play the Omnichord, an
electronic musical instrument from
the 80s. The songs include her voice
as well as electronic music. Each piece
is named the date it was composed.

A ROOM
WITH A VOICE

Hans asked two cellists, a clarinetist
and a violinist to each choose a space
in the museum, listen to the sounds
that are present, and improvise
something that suited the location.
As documentation, each musician
made a video of their performance,
the music piece was written as a score,
and the location they played was
marked on a floor plan. Afterwards,
the scores were sung by a male bass
and a female soprano in Hans's studio.
The voice often can't sing the
same notes as the instruments,
so the pieces had to be interpreted.
The music was further affected by
the space because each location had
its own sound. Despite the differences
between the instruments and the
voices, and between the architecture
of the museum and Hans's studio,
this work connects the spaces both
physically and mentally. Although
creative work is normally developed
in the studio and moved to the museum,
it's the opposite case in this piece.

INCOMPLETE NEIGHBOR
Raffaella Crispino and
Hans Demeulenaere
Onomatopee #240

First edition: 2023

Published by Onomatopee
ISBN 978-94-93148-93-2

Graphic Design
    Bureau Vielcazat
Typeface
    Schotis Text
Paper
    Magno Volume
    Arena White Rough
    Constellation Snow
Copies
    500

This publication is made on
the occasion of the exhibition
'Incomplete Neighbor'
at the Petach Tikva Museum of Art,
Petach-Tikva, Israel
June 1 - October 31, 2023

Project's initiator and creator
of the exhibition's concept
    Nirith Nelson

Exhibition Curator
    Tal Bechler

Petach Tikva Museum of Art
Director
    Reut Ferster
Chief Curator
    Irena Gordon

Editor
    Jesse Muller

Contributing authors
    Tal Bechler
    Raffaella Crispino
    Hans Demeulenaere

English translation and editing
    Daria Kassovsky
    Emi Kodama

Photography
    Dieter Van Caneghem
    Raffaella Crispino

Digitalisation
    Fotorama, Ghent (B)

Printer
    Graphius, Ghent (B)

Made possible by the
generous support of:

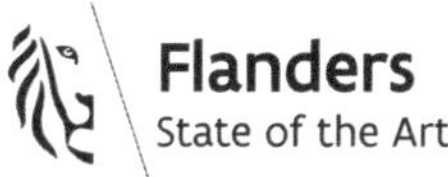
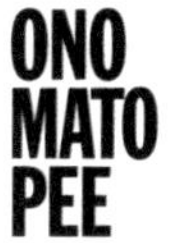
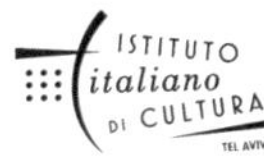

Special thanks to:

Eva Maria Bouillon
Erik Buchberger
Benoit Burquel
Gert De Clercq
Aude Cliquennois
Griet De Geyter
Tamar Deutsch
Michael Langeder
Caroline Lonneville
Peter Jacob Maltz
Michal Oren
Shira Pinkerfeld
Adriana Rispoli
Naama Serfaty
Alberta Sessa
Maria Sica
Thomas Vanlede
Robbe Vancraeynest

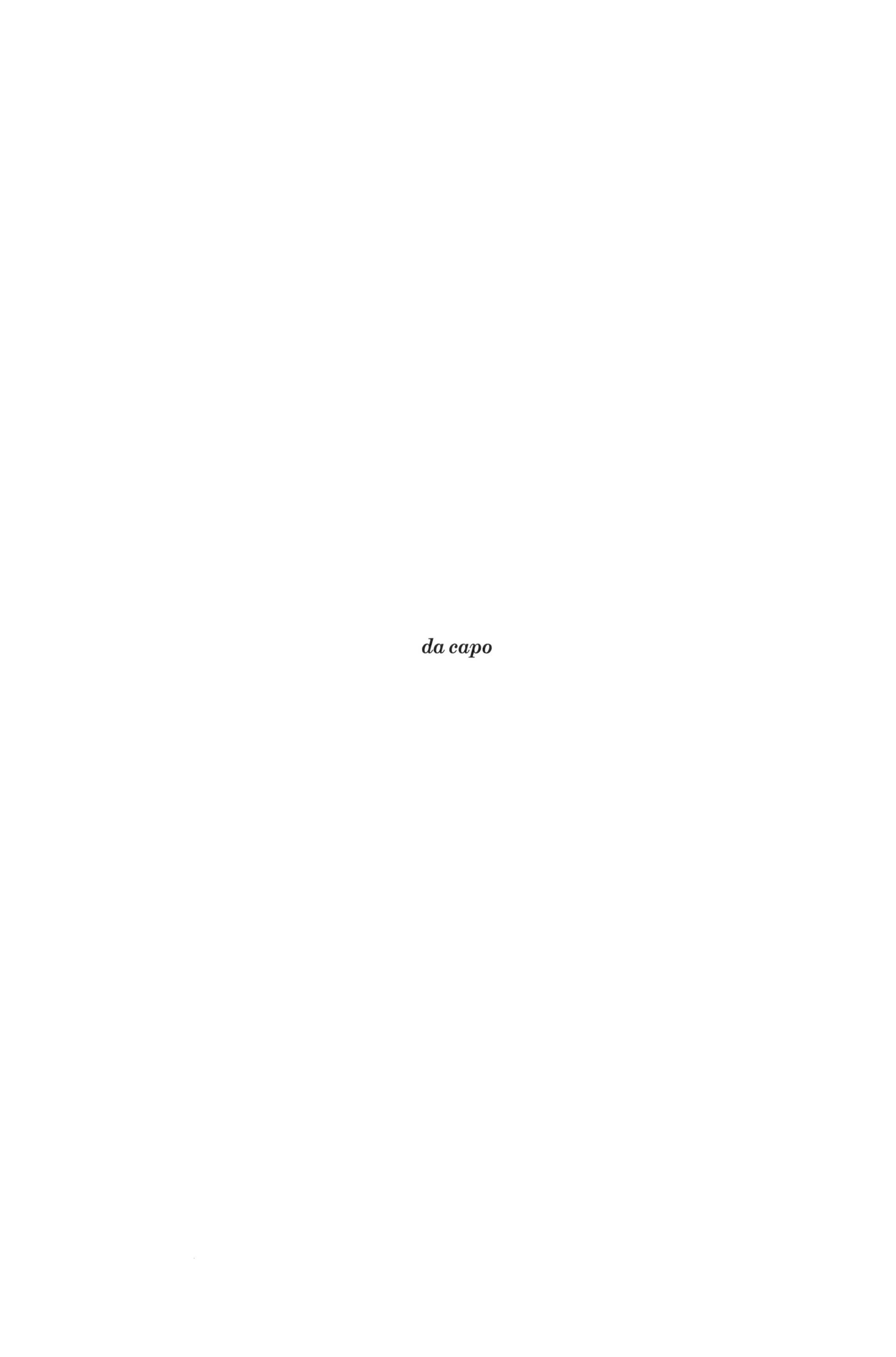

da capo

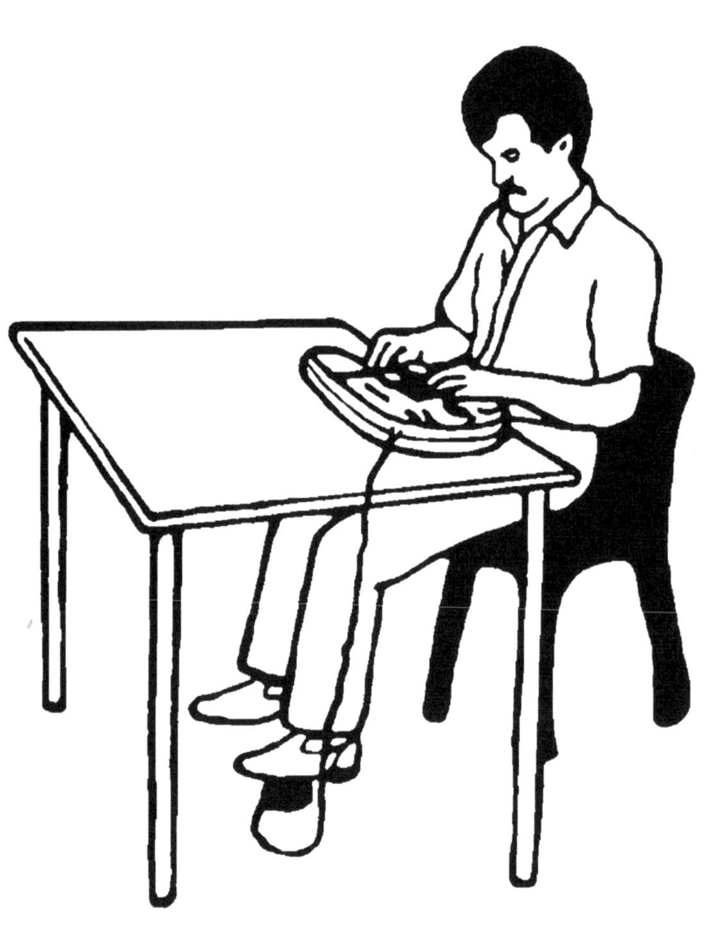